FROM THE LAKE HOUSE

FROM THE
LAKE HOUSE

A MOTHER'S ODYSSEY
OF LOSS AND LOVE

A Memoir

KRISTEN RADEMACHER

SHE WRITES PRESS

AUTHOR'S NOTE

In shaping this memoir, I relied on my early journal entries and my unpublished essays about losing a baby. I also drew from the shifting sands of my memory and perceptions—especially in writing dialogue—and from the recollections of friends and family who supported me in those early days. Except for those of my family, most names in this memoir have been changed to preserve privacy. To form a cohesive narrative flow, I formed a couple of composite characters by merging traits from several people, and I collapsed several incidents from the true chronology of events into single scenes.

Published 2020
Printed in the United States of America
ISBN: 978-1-63152-866-8
ISBN: 978-1-63152-867-5
Library of Congress Control Number: 2020900201

For information, address:
She Writes Press
1569 Solano Ave #546
Berkeley, CA 94707

Interior design by Tabitha Lahr

She Writes Press is a division of SparkPoint Studio, LLC.

For Carly

Your body is away from me
But there is a window open
from my heart to yours.
From this window, like the moon
I keep sending news secretly.

—Rumi

CONTENTS

~~~~~~~

Chapter 1—DOCK

Lowering myself to my bedroom's cool tile floor, I leaned against the cornflower blue wall, pulled my knees into my chest, and looked around. A dust bunny, carried by a breeze streaming in through the open window, floated past my ankles and landed in front of two canvas bags. The movers had hauled away furniture and boxes and lamps and plants, and all that was left in my house was my elderly cat cowering in the bathroom. And these bags.

A jewelry box in one bag housed dangly beaded earrings, silver necklaces, a few pendants, and one string of pearls, a gift from an ex-boyfriend. I'd worn the pearls at cocktail parties and swanky restaurants when I'd lived in Boston, but they'd never left the velvet-lined drawer after moving to Chapel Hill. Though unnecessary and frankly silly, I had safeguarded my modest assortment of trinkets and ornaments from a ride in the moving truck.

A small birch picture frame poked out of the second bag. Behind the glass was a set of tiny footprints, and inching myself closer, I tried looking at them with new eyes, hoping to uncover something different about the pattern on the heels and big toe mounds, or the way the toes were nearly perfectly spaced apart. But

1

I couldn't. I'd stared at them too often, their image permanently etched in my mind. The frame used to sit on the windowsill beside a pink bowl where I kept two Polaroids, our hospital bracelets, the ultrasound photo, and several seashells I'd fervently gathered for her on a Florida beach after the good-bye. The bowl lay carefully wrapped in the bag, along with a floral hatbox stuffed with condolence cards, one small diaper, and my plum-colored journal filled with letters to her and reflections on how to keep living.

No way would movers' hands touch the homage to my daughter. I was carrying it myself.

"I should get out of here," I said aloud. "The movers will wonder where I am."

Facing the bank of windows, my eyes followed the gently rolling lawn, past the weeping willow and the dogwoods, past the patches of azaleas and hydrangeas, down to the water. I'd been renting this simple basement apartment of a beautiful home that sat on the shoreline of a small lake. It was here where I'd discovered that the outdoors held magic, that birdsongs could uplift, and that amber and golden leaves swirling in circles on a windswept fall morning could astonish with their sun-dappled dance. It was here where I no longer dreaded the swoop of emptiness descending like a fast-moving fog—my breath suddenly shallow, chest tight, body wanting to curl up like a potato bug. I learned to yield to sorrow and retreat to my easy chair, or the patio next to the rose bushes, or the dock where ripples of water weaved through my toes. Part of me longed to extend my lease on the apartment because it was here where I'd stopped spinning. Finally, enfolded in the peaceful solitude of the lake house, I had looked inside myself, cultivated roots, and begun to heal.

"Are you ready, Max?"

My voice echoed through the empty rooms. My gray tuxedo cat eyed me from behind the toilet where he'd spent the day. He was still adjusting to life without his beloved brother whom I'd recently buried out back near the gardenias. "It's okay, little boy." I rubbed the white patch beneath his chin. "You'll like the new house." As I turned to leave, I caught my reflection in the mirror. "And you'll like it too." My cheeks were flushed, and shadows under my eyes showed fatigue from a late night of packing. I was forty-three years old and moving into the first place I'd ever bought, a freshly reno-vated townhouse with a brand-new kitchen and bathrooms and a secluded stone patio lined with crape myrtles. A home all my own.

I scooped Max into my arms and tucked his head into the crook of my neck. He refused to purr, refused to look at me. "I'm sorry for another move," I whispered into his downy ear, "but this will be it for a while. Promise."

Should he believe me after the cascade of changes and losses? Impulsively relocating to Chapel Hill had not unfolded as I'd expected. Then again, what *had* I expected? With little forethought, had I really hoped to flee Boston and my broken heart and slide like warm butter into a new and improved romance, an upgraded life in the South? Had I been naïve, desperate, unlucky? Perhaps all three?

I stood at the dock one last time before placing Max and the canvas bags in my aged Jetta. The air was warm for mid-March, and sunlight skipped along the lake's surface. A lone woman in a kayak glided by, stroke slow and steady, her red hat a burst of color against the still, pewter water. I watched until she disappeared. A mere two years earlier on a chilly January afternoon, I had moved by myself into this apartment after my life as I'd known it had all but disappeared. Like a busted-up jigsaw puzzle, pieces of it had been scattered about, a few gone missing, and somehow I had to make myself whole again.

Chapter 2—Jason

My courtship with Jason had begun five years earlier and not until after we'd moved in together. He'd flown up to Boston, helped me load a truck with everything I owned, two cats included, and we'd driven it all to North Carolina. Three days later, set up in our newly rented Chapel Hill cottage, we celebrated the Fourth of July. I loved the irony of this. Freedom! Jason and I sat side by side in lawn chairs on our front deck, fingers clasped and a beer balancing in each of our laps. *No more endless winters*, I thought. No more herding fifth graders, no more desperate speculation about what had gone wrong with Brian.

"Here's to new beginnings," I said, raising my bottle to clink Jason's.

He leaned in to kiss me, and then we sat back and listened to the booms from distant fireworks. Closing my eyes, I breathed in the sweet scent of magnolias wafting up to us from the huge tree beyond the deck. Fist-sized white magnolia blooms are uncommon in New England, as are kudzu-covered pine trees, and coral and periwinkle crape myrtle blossoms. My new landscape seemed like talismans of my new life.

I'm a planner—careful, systematic. So when I'd told my friends and family that I was leaving my teaching job, my apartment, the city I'd lived in for more than a dozen years for North Carolina, they'd stared at me. What? And when I told them that Jason and I were going to live together, their mouths fell open. He and I had known each other for a whopping six months and, save for a handful of weekend visits, our long-distance history had consisted of phone calls and email. Surely I might want to take things more slowly? But I didn't. At thirty-eight, slow and steady wasn't working.

When I'd met Jason, I was reeling. My ex-boyfriend Brian, a Boston attorney I had been involved with for three years, that blue-eyed, blond-haired, Irish-Catholic, sports-loving family man, the one I was so certain I'd marry and have a kid or two with, had royally dumped me—and on 9/11. I was out of my mind with misery for months, slumped in my apartment amid a constant flow of tears and wine, until at Christmas I crash-landed at my brother's farmhouse near Chapel Hill, beyond grateful to get out of my bleak head and bitter cold Boston. Who did I happen to meet during my holiday getaway? Jason. An easygoing, boot-wearing, homegrown North Carolinian, staggering from his recent divorce. We were a match made in Rebound Heaven. We grabbed ahold of each other like Velcro and didn't let go.

We called our house a nest. It sat on the crest of a shady hill, and we lived on top of each other in the small rooms. That suited us just fine as we settled into the hot summer filled with love and lust and the belief that together we were going to build a great new life. We entwined our legs when lazing on the sofa and locked hands when running errands. Sometimes Jason and I moved the furniture to the side of our living room, turned the stereo up, and danced, his hazel eyes smiling and long, lean limbs swaying against mine. He'd occasionally lift me off the floor and twirl my lithe, petite frame, our laughter as loud as the music, and when he set me back down, he'd brush wisps of my fine hair off my cheeks.

With a history of general contract work and also all-around handy and creative, Jason had left his decorative concrete business post-divorce to design and construct green, sustainable buildings. That summer he was hard at work on his first house and believed more would follow, the start of a prosperous new business. Before Jason left for the day, off to the countryside with his work crew, I'd start coffee and breakfast. After the last bite of our bagels, we'd kiss good-bye at the kitchen door.

"See you tonight, sweetie," he'd say, "and call me if you get lonely."

"Okay." I'd smile back at him, leaning into his chest. "What do you want for dinner? Actually, never mind. I'll surprise you."

And we'd kiss one more time, as if our morning ritual was the most normal thing in the world, as if we'd been doing it our whole lives, and I'd wave to Jason as he drove off.

Without another year of teaching looming ahead, nothing lay in front of me professionally but a vague notion about finding a new path in education. Not having a clear direction was a strange place for me. Back when I was twenty-three, my decision to teach had hit me with such Road to Damascus clarity that I couldn't believe I'd wasted my first year out of college without seeing my obvious path. I'd gotten myself into a top graduate program, waitressed my way through a master's degree, and landed a plum teaching position in one of Massachusetts's best public schools. For a long time I'd thrived, so attached to my students I couldn't bear to be out sick. Parents clamored to get their kids into my class, and I had plenty of teacher friends to join for happy hours on Fridays, ski trips in the winter, and beach trips in the summer. I had a good life.

I floated through my first Chapel Hill summer with boisterous fifth graders, Boston, and Brian behind me. Having no plans of any kind and with some money saved, I felt no pressure to rush a job search. I loved my virtual anonymity in Chapel Hill and savored the rare gift of unstructured time. Sometimes I took long walks through my new neighborhood, shopped for household supplies, or chipped away at more unpacking. I sent emails to my friends back in Boston and wrote in my journal. My poor journal had been the repository of my anger and anguish the previous year, multitudes of entries about Brian. *How could he have left?* I asked its pages again and again. *He doesn't even explain. Just disappears.* Entries about 9/11. *All those souls pulverized to ash*, I wrote. *The terror they must have felt.* How many nights had I sat numbly in front of the television, watching the image of the crumbling Twin Towers? My childhood home was less than fifty miles away, across the Sound on Long Island. I had grown up seeing those towers materialize on the horizon as the train I'd take to Manhattan approached the city. *Everything is chaos*, I had scrawled across my journal's pages. *Brian won't return my calls. Lower Manhattan's a graveyard. I don't want to teach anymore.*

Fast forward to my North Carolina nest. *I'm here!!!* I wrote with extra exclamation marks. *This little house is so sweet. And so is Jason.*

And he was. I'd make the bed in the morning to discover a love note tucked under my pillow. He'd spontaneously grab me around my waist, hold my face in his hands, and tell me that he loved me. He'd offer back rubs, bring home chocolate, and crack me up with his hilarious impressions of North Carolina politicians.

That summer we found lakes and ponds for swimming on the weekends, ate dinner on the front lawn of the local co-op, and visited my brother out on his farm. We rode our bicycles through nearby wooded trails, dumbfounded one evening after discovering we were lost. Light dwindling, we sheepishly asked directions from a friendly hiker and then laughed at ourselves all the way home.

One August afternoon, we drove half a day for an im-promptu trip to the Outer Banks, found a spit of nearly deserted beach, and pitched a tent. After swimming and languishing until the sun dropped out of view, we sat on beach chairs next to our tent, buried our feet in the sand, ate tuna sandwiches, and drank tepid beer. Jason pulled me onto his lap and we kissed; all I could hear was the sound of the surf and our own breathing.

"Isn't this great?" Jason asked. "I know it's only been a couple of months, but we're really doing this, aren't we?"

"Yeah, we are." We high-fived each other. "Who would have thought that a northern city girl and a southern country boy would fall in love and do so well together?"

And we did. Every time we stumbled into a cultural chasm, we simply climbed out and kept going. I didn't give a second thought to the fact that the novels and authors I read were com-pletely unknown to him. I ignored the fact that he set the radio to country music while I kept switching it back to NPR. That hunting rifle he kept in the shed didn't represent a clash of life-styles, did it? Nor did the multiple deer racks his parents proudly displayed in their home? We shared stories of our adolescence, and I found the contrast charming. He'd worn camouflage gear with his dad, waiting up in a tree for an unsuspecting deer to amble by, or cheered at NASCAR races, or dealt weed in the shadows of his high school. I'd played my violin, attended Broadway plays, and kept company with my high school's nerdy theater crowd. And while I took the higher education route after high school, earning bachelor's and master's degrees from preppy New England schools, Jason had gone directly to work, first for his father at a manufacturing plant, and then bouncing from job to job.

On paper we might have been an unlikely couple, but I didn't care. Sure, I'd spent more time deliberating over the color of a new sofa than I had in choosing to uproot myself and partner with Jason. But his steady stream of affection felt soothing, like good southern molasses, and it brought me back to life. And all the newness of Chapel Hill—the geography, the house, the accents, and the flora—was exactly the balm I needed to release the despair and tumult of my ending with Brian.

Chapter 3—BOSTON

Less than a year before my arrival in Chapel Hill, I had been utterly enamored and happily coupled with Brian. Had a crystal ball portended that we wouldn't end up together, that I'd leave Boston and start over in the South with another man, I would have guffawed at the preposterous forecast. Boston was my home. My future with Brian was solid as granite.

I'd routinely make the Friday night drive up Boston's highway to see him. Fresh out of a shower with blond hair still wet, Brian would greet me with a glass of wine and a flirtatious smile.

"Do you think I need a second bathroom?" he'd ask after a soft kiss.

"You absolutely do need a second bathroom," I'd play along. "*And* more closets."

We'd plop onto his sumptuous leather sofa. "I don't know." He'd wink his steel blue eyes. "Why do I need extra space?"

"Because." I'd gesture to my overnight bag tossed by the staircase. "There's nowhere to put my stuff."

"Oh, right." Brian would settle our wine glasses on the coffee table so he could pull me into his thick torso and wrap his arms around me. "Your stuff would look kinda cute next to mine."

A few kisses and emptied wine glasses later, we'd head out for the evening. Snapshots of our three years together show us eating in harbor-view restaurants, cheering at Celtic games, and enjoying concerts. We cruised Boston's North Shore in his fishing boat and shared weekends with his family on a lake in Maine. We traveled to Mexico, Dominican Republic, Paris.

But he never did fix up his house, and our clothes never shared a closet. As we started our third year together, I was ready to discuss commitment for real, but Brian grew distant.

And then 9/11.

I imagine the terror of that day pushed Brian over the edge, and he decided that with all those lost lives, he might as well get lost too. The towers fell and he simply stopped calling. I left him voice mails and emails imploring him to get in touch. Radio silence. After a week, he managed one short message on my answering machine.

"I'm confused. I need space and time to think."

And in the weeks and months that ensued, I endured long days teaching lackluster lessons to my prepubescent charges, my stomach coiled in knots, the lump in my throat threatening tears, my mind desperately trying to focus. Evenings, I'd call girlfriends or my mother. They unanimously agreed that if Brian could discard me like a used newspaper, I was better off without him. At first I wanted him back; then I wanted an explanation. I'd fall asleep on my sofa after one last gulp of merlot and relish the few breaths of no-memory when I first awoke in the morning, a brief reprieve before thoughts of Brian flooded my mind.

My despondency turned to disgust when Brian sent me a generic Christmas card and a poinsettia, the type of impersonal gift he likely doled out to his law clients. I finally snapped.

"Asshole!" I seethed. "Shithead! Go to hell!" I ripped up Brian's card and booked a flight to North Carolina to visit my brother for the holidays.

The sun was shining when my plane touched down for my North Carolina, Brian-Breakup Holiday Retreat. I traded in my winter coat for a fleece sweatshirt, sat outside, and watched my six-year-old nephew jump on his trampoline. Hawks flew overhead, swooping through the pastures and woods that my brother and a dozen other households called home. The sun beat down on my face, and for the first time in months, I did not feel claustrophobic. Away from my noisy classroom, the cold leaden sky, my small grief-gobbed apartment, the nonstop news of 9/11—I could finally breathe.

It was on an afternoon walk when I ran into a tall, slender man with almond-shaped eyes, chiseled cheekbones, and a base-ball cap atop his sandy brown hair.

"Hi there." He stuck his hand out to shake mine. "I'm Jason."

"I'm Kristen, David's sister. Visiting from Boston."

He told me he was visiting too, but from a few counties over.

"I'm actually renting a cabin here. Getting divorced. Need a place to crash for a while."

"Ouch," I said.

"No kidding. And the cabin is the size of a card table."

His chestnut cowboy boots caught my eye as I laughed.

And what should have been an innocuous meeting with a fellow guest at the farm changed my life forever.

I walked daily through the fields and trails, grateful for the temperate climate and bucolic countryside. On one jaunt I saw Jason in front of a small cluster of homes. He raised his arm and waved me over.

"Hey," he said when I reached him. "Care for a cup of tea? I've got an electric kettle in my place." He motioned to what looked like a shed.

A twin bed, a table, and two folding chairs filled his Lilliputian cabin. Jason sat back in his chair, legs outstretched before him so that his feet rubbed up against the base of the bed. It felt odd being close enough to this unknown man to see his jeans worn at the knees and frayed along the ankles, and his bare, trim torso peeking out from his untucked corduroy shirt. We talked about the farm, 9/11, and our respective breakup stories.

"You won't have any trouble getting out there again," Jason said, looking squarely into my eyes. "Someone will snatch you up."

My cheeks darkened.

Before the end of my trip, Jason invited me to dinner. *A date!* I thought. *Take that, Brian!* Over pasta and wine at a small Italian restaurant, Jason talked confidently about his dreams to design green buildings, and I talked about tiring of teaching. The flickering candle on the table and the buzz from the wine made Jason's eyes sparkle. In his truck after dinner, he leaned in and kissed me sweetly and briefly, his mustache soft against my lips.

"Brian was a fool to let you go," he whispered.

Jason called a few weeks later after I was back in frigid New England.

"Your brother gave me your number. Want a visitor?"

He was interested in checking out Boston's architecture, or so he said. He told me he'd stay in my spare room. "But by all means, say no if this seems strange."

"Sure, why not," I said. "Come on up." I reasoned that I could use a jump start to get out again after my heartsick autumn.

"I'm *not* looking for a new boyfriend," I told a friend. "I'll be glad for the company."

"Right." She smirked.

Jason visited on a blustery January weekend, and after an awkward pickup from the airport (*my God*, I thought, struggling to make conversation, *what in the hell am I doing?*), we relaxed. I showed him around Cambridge, took him to my favorite bar and museum. His enthusiasm was infectious: he loved the city's energy, the mix of historical and modern neighborhoods, and the winding Charles River. By the second evening, snow was falling steadily, and we stayed in. Sprawled on my living room floor, we polished off a bottle of wine, sampled my music collection, and enjoyed long, tender kisses. I couldn't help but note the contrast in my state of being. Before Christmas, I'd hated being at home, hated being at school, hated being awake. And here I was, lazing with an easygoing southern man while music filled my home and fluffy snowflakes drifted past my windows. I felt buoyant, which made sleeping with him seem natural despite my history of keeping suitors at a safe distance. *Fuck it all*, I'd thought, flushed with wine and delight that the months of gloom were gone. *I don't care.* And I didn't care, not even when Jason told me that he'd campaigned for Ross Perot a few elections back (*huh? that buffoon?*), and not when his cowboy boots lying askew beside my bed looked wrong in Boston's light of day.

Jason kissed me good-bye in front of the airport terminal. I wrapped my scarf a little closer against my neck, pulled my hat over my ears, and smiled. Jason got on the plane and flew away, and I was still smiling. I savored the newfound release of pain, as if after walking uphill in tight heels on concrete for miles, I was finally strolling barefoot across plush grass. Nothing could stop the feeling, not a farewell to Jason who lived eight states away, and not returning home to my empty house where I'd ached for months over Brian. My body felt peaceful, my mind tranquil, and for the first time in forever, sleep came easily and deep.

And then the phone rang and rang, yanking me from a dream.

"Kristen." I heard a man's voice on the end of the line.

"Who is this?" I whispered into my pitch-black bedroom. The clock read one in the morning.

"It's Brian. I'm sorry to wake you. Sorry for everything."

And then he started weeping, his apologies and sobs a jumble of sounds I could barely follow. He'd been missing since September, but on this January night, and for the next three months, Brian committed himself to repairing the mess he'd made with us. He sent flowers to my school and my house. Sent cards filled with explanations, remorse, and pleadings for forgiveness. He left voice mails asking to see me, wrote an apology letter to my mother, probably sat his Catholic self in a pew of his parish and prayed.

Seems Brian had decided that he was cured from whatever had pushed him away. His long absence had been a mere pause in our relationship, and we only needed to press play and resume. In the few phone calls I took from Brian during this time, I told him in no uncertain terms that we were finished, but privately mourned our dissolution all over again. We'd loved each other, hadn't we? How had our love ended up in tatters? Would I ever have what my friends had: standard courtships and stable marriages and the underlying security of a united front? I wondered if relationship uncertainty was hardwired into my DNA.

My parents' first separation lasted less than twenty-four hours. I was twelve when my father told me at breakfast that he was leaving my mother. Then he drove me to school. I walked mutely through the halls of junior high and kept my shooting stomach pains to myself. My weary-looking mother was in bed when I got home and said that my father had decided to stay after all. He'd changed his mind, I guess, and if my parents explained this to me, I don't recall.

What I do remember is spending the rest of my adolescence on edge, growing vigilant because how was I to know if my parents were faking it, or anyone else for that matter? Five years later, my father left for good. He delivered the news at breakfast again, this time the morning after my high school graduation. He moved out two weeks later. And in the months that followed, I left for my first semester of college, my father introduced my brothers and me to his future new wife, and my mother essentially became a single parent to my younger brother. My family as I'd known us, a moderately happy clan of five under one roof, had vanished.

While Brian ran a relentless campaign to win me back, Jason kept in touch. He phoned again and again after our snowy Boston weekend, his cheerful voice and descriptions of sunny and warm North Carolina an antidote to Brian's steady and sappy voice mails and the barren trees outside my window. I had no vision of a future with Jason but giggled at his jokes and raves about the virtues of green building.

It was April when Brian, in his last-ditch effort to get back together, showed up in my school's parking lot, kids and parents loitering nearby in their end-of-the-day conversations.

"Can we talk?" he nervously pleaded, standing in front of my car in a tan suit, not one strand of his golden hair out of place.

"No," I whispered.

And that's when he pulled a black velvet box out of his pocket, knelt down, and proposed marriage, hoping a sparkling diamond ring would shake my resolve. I told him to stand the hell up and stop, shooting a quick glance at the curious parents and children.

"You're too late," I murmured as he rose from his knees. "Far too late."

I got into my car, started the engine, and pulled away.

"Where was he when I needed him?" I sobbed to a friend as I paced my kitchen, phone in one hand and glass of merlot in the other. "Why now, after all these months?"

Jason suggested I come to North Carolina for a visit. "North Carolina is beautiful in spring, and don't you have a school vacation coming up?"

The sky was a piercing blue on each day of that trip, and Jason promised, as we strolled Chapel Hill's botanical gardens, that the cacophony of colors—vibrant greens on the budding trees and shrubs, and loads of pastel pink and purple azalea blooms—were not at all unusual. "This is springtime in North Carolina, sweetheart!" Jason said with such zeal that I threw my arms around him. Our visit was nearly perfect: we lingered over coffee each morning on his small deck amid an anthem of birdsongs, barbecued with my brother, and walked through the university's stately campus.

By June's end I'd traded my friends, a desirable job, a city I loved in liberal-minded, quick-witted, fast-paced New England for the lush greenery of a quaint, southern university town. I'd simply walked away from the epicenter of my heartbreak and plunged into the unknown with Jason.

Chapter 4—DEBT

———～·～———

"You almost declared bankruptcy?" I asked. "When?"
Jason and I were home on a Saturday evening, three months into our cohabitation, when he told me he didn't have money for dinner out.

"Kris," he frowned. "Let's talk."

And that's when I learned that as Jason's marriage fell apart, he had accrued serious credit-card debt, come close to filing for Chapter 11, but had decided to chip away at the thousands of dollars owed instead. He wasn't close to making a dent in his bills. His general contractor's license had also expired; during the chaos of his divorce, he had watched as the deadline to reapply came and went.

We sat next to each other on the couch looking straight ahead. "But you're building a house now?" I asked. "How is that possible?"

He explained that, while uncommon, some clients hired builders without a license. It was cheaper for them. And when I asked why he didn't just go ahead and get his renewed, he said that he didn't have the necessary proof of assets. But he promised that after wrapping up the house, he'd find more building projects, pay off his debt, and start saving.

I could have reacted to Jason's confession with anger. Why had he withheld important information about his finances until well *after* I'd moved? Why hadn't I asked more questions before I jumped into this new life? I could have taken the opportunity to wonder if my move was somewhat . . . rash. I could have seen Jason's admission as a cautionary tale and wondered what else I didn't know about him.

But I did none of that. Instead, I watched a small, innocent seed of judgment about Jason hover near me. Rather than push it away, I let it sink into soil. *Well, that was foolish.* And then I appointed myself CFO of our relationship and took over all the finances, something I'd always known how to do.

———

I was the kid in my family with jobs and cash. Every day after junior high, I loaded my three-speed bicycle with dozens of papers, and my skinny preteen legs pedaled through the streets bringing news of Long Island to my neighbors. I was the neighborhood babysitter. In high school I ran the register at two different pharmacies. Sold burgers at a fast-food restaurant. Tutored. An arthritic housebound widow hired me for an array of chores she could no longer manage. I mowed her lawn, weeded her garden, picked up thinly sliced salami at the deli and light bulbs at the hardware store. I kept my earnings stuffed in a small box in my desk's top drawer, and in the days before ATM machines, I often spotted my parents cash until they could get to a bank. Sometimes I'd simply find a note in the box: *IOU $20. Love, Mom.*

By the time I'd established myself in Boston, I was a creditor's dream: reasonable savings, no debt. And in my three years with Brian, our only discussion of money was when I tried to occasionally pick up the dinner tab. He almost always refused. "I got this," he'd insist. From concerts to movies to vacations, Brian covered it all. He earned much more as an attorney than I did as a teacher, so I eventually relaxed into this arrangement.

~~

After Jason revealed the truth of his financial status, I put all the bills in my name and paid them from my account each month, Jason reimbursing me what he could. The notion of Jason picking up the bill after a shared dinner or the two of us sharing a bank account never came up.

It didn't take me long to find work in Chapel Hill. Because I'd spent my entire life in school, either as a student or a teacher, I wandered into the university's temporary employment office in the fall and within a week was placed as a receptionist in the academic support department. *Perfect*, I thought, when I discovered they also had an unfilled position for a learning specialist. While I answered phones and greeted students coming into the office, I made sure to share my education background with the director. Before long I applied for and was hired as the learning specialist. The appointment was only three-quarters time, but it was a start. So, along with the three other women in the department, I began helping undergraduates shore up their academic skills. I also began collecting benefits and earning a salary again.

Compared to my former traffic-filled commute down a Boston highway, a day teaching spirited children, and an evening of grading homework, I welcomed the change of my new working life. Each morning I rode the bus from my neighborhood into the heart of town, several blocks lined with T-shirt shops, coffee houses, and cheap eateries for students. I walked across the brick pathways of the campus, oak trees towering overhead, and smiled at the teeming backpack-toting twenty-somethings. I had energy and free time after work, and I cooked full dinners for Jason and me, read, took walks in the warm autumn temperatures, and was delighted by Halloween pumpkins sitting beside still-blooming pansies.

Jason, meanwhile, tried to generate momentum for his nascent business. If enthusiasm alone were enough to help it grow, he would have succeeded, as his extroverted, cheerful personality invited conversation everywhere we went. We'd stand in line for movie tickets, and inevitably Jason would share his passion for sustainable building with the couple behind us. He constantly showed me photos of homes made from rammed earth or straw bale or other earth-friendly materials. "Aren't they beautiful?" he'd ask. Years earlier, Jason had charmed his way into an apprenticeship in Arizona to learn specialized skills of alternative building construction. One cold call to the head architect was all it took for Jason to get free airfare, meals, and a place to stay in exchange for working alongside the lead engineer.

But without a general contractor's license, I couldn't help but wonder if Jason's dream of growing a green-building venture was doomed. How would he ever get enough big jobs that paid the big bucks?

And how would all of this impact me?

As Thanksgiving approached, Jason collected his final payment on the house he built. I asked him over dinner one evening about future projects.

"I'm building a screened-in porch," he said.

"When do you start?"

Jason gulped his beer, pushed his chair back, and walked to the fridge. The beginnings of a hole had formed at the knee of his worn, faded jeans, and as he leaned into the fridge to grab a second beer, I noticed another hole forming on his back pocket. Jason's work attire consisted of shabby clothes, and they got so dirty that we kept them segregated from the rest of the laundry.

At first I loved the newness of this. Men I'd known did not earn livings with their hands, build things, and end their day with exhausted bodies. My father, an engineer, wore a suit day after day. Brian also wore suits, or pleated trousers with button-down shirts, as did his brothers, my brothers, the principal of the school where I'd taught, and my male co-teachers. The working men I'd known didn't sweat and toil during the day, and while their professional wardrobe hung in a closet, Jason's lay in a heap in the laundry room, cats' litter box a few feet away.

Jason returned to the table, cold beer in hand. "I just need to get over there, take measurements, and order lumber," he said. "Does it matter when I start?"

"Well, yeah. The sooner you start, the sooner you'll get paid." I sipped my water and noticed Jason's hair was getting that shaggy, needing-a-trim look.

"I know you're worried, but don't." Jason patted my knee. "I'll build the damn porch, I'll get paid, and I'll build lots more if I need to. But I also need time to write my business plan and finish my website."

Jason spent hours tweaking his website, hoping to lure potential investors, and he was so certain that with careful and consistent marketing, his next big house venture was just around the corner. No mere porches for him. He gave cards away to anyone with hands, from people we'd meet walking the trails to the cashier at the grocery store. I rooted for him, but my practical self, the one who took charge of budgeting and shopping, simply wanted to stay in the black each month.

So, when Jason headed down the hall to his office in the evenings after dinner, I hoped he would make calls and hustle up a few more home improvement jobs. Sometimes he did, but he also wiled away his time in never-ending website revisions. I was troubled by Jason's seeming lack of urgency to pay off his debt, and by his seeming ease at contributing less than me to our expenses each month. *I'm the primary breadwinner yet earn a part-time salary*, I often contemplated as I curled in bed reading, waiting for Jason to log off his computer and join me.

How long could we pull off this arrangement?

Chapter 5—SHRINKING

~~~~~~~~

Walking into my house after work one drab January after-noon, I glanced into my kitchen. What a mess: last night's dirty pan still on the stove, an open box of breakfast cereal on the counter, an unfinished bagel with hardened cream cheese on a dish. Looks like I'd have to clean the kitchen again before making dinner. Tossing my bags on a table, I poured myself a glass of wine and held the first sip on my tongue before letting it slide down my throat. My view out the kitchen window was a patch of pine trees and a small brick ranch house, similar to mine and all the others in my neighborhood. My neighborhood outside of Boston had been made up of thick hardwoods and multifamily two- and three-story houses. I closed my eyes and pictured myself in my old apartment, marking fifth-grade math homework, reading the *Boston Globe*, making plans on the phone with a friend for the coming weekend. I felt a sudden and strong ache for my old single life. When was the last time I'd wandered a city street, sipped wine at a bar with girlfriends, had a reason to dress up?

I couldn't help but note that compared to my life in Bos-ton—a school filled with friends, more restaurants than I could ever sample, enough culture to interest me forever—my new world had shrunk. It used to be that I'd travel hours to visit a parent or a sibling. No longer. My brother David, his fiancée Kate, and my six-year-old nephew had moved out of their farmhouse and bought a home across from mine and Jason's, giving me one less reason to venture out of Chapel Hill's city limits. For the first time since I'd left home for college, family was within eyesight. Literally. David and I chatted from our driveways. I'd logged plenty of miles on my car when I lived in Boston: driving the highway to my school, to friends scattered throughout the greater metropolitan area, to nearby Cape Cod, New Hampshire, Maine, and Vermont. Here, I worked less than ten minutes from home, and the few friends I had all lived nearby. My entire world revolved within a five-mile radius.

My bank account had also shrunk. My three-quarter-position salary covered the household expenses and little else, Jason contributing what he earned from small construction and carpentry projects he found. We were always just getting by, never accruing enough of a buffer to eat out more often, attend occasional concerts, or splurge on a weekend trip. "As soon as I sign on to build another house," Jason kept promising, "things will get easier."

My cats wedged themselves beside me on the easy chair where I'd settled with my wine and the day's pile of mail. Tucked among the bills was a greeting card from a friend back home. Along with a cheery note, she'd included a photo of herself standing next to her snow-covered car: *I bet you don't miss this!* She was right. How often had I layered myself in wool sweaters and a down parka to brave the howling wind and bitter cold? How many feet of snow had I shoveled from my driveway and scraped off my car during my tenure in New England? I'd endured winter after winter, counting down those final dreary weeks of March until tender green buds would finally brighten the interminable colorless landscape. As I stared at the photo, I didn't miss fierce nor'easters, but somehow the sight of my friend's mittens, hat, and rosy, wind-kissed cheeks made my yearning for all that I'd left behind grow stronger.

"It's normal to sometimes miss my old life, right?" I asked my cats. I wanted to slip on a dress, heels, and jewelry, put on lipstick, and go to a big production of a hot new play. Venues like the ones I'd visit in Boston did not exist in Chapel Hill, however, and even if they did, our tight budget restricted such doings. I had been far from wealthy as a teacher, but I'd had greater financial freedom and routinely selected from a full slate of social events and activities.

"But," I told my cats while returning the photo to the envelope, "I'm building a new life, right here, in North Carolina. In a perfectly lovely university town. With Jason." They opened their eyes and turned up the volume of their purr.

As if I needed instant reassurance about my decision to leave Boston, Jason walked through the back door, whistling a cheerful melody.

"Hi, sweetheart." He grinned, standing in front of me with his hands behind his back. "I have two surprises for you."

And he handed me a small bunch of tulips and a pizza pie.

"Nice combination, huh?" He laughed. "I know you want to try that new Thai restaurant, but for now, let's enjoy our favorite pizza."

"Oh, Jason." I kissed him. "Your timing is perfect. Thank you."

"And the flowers are because I love you. And for hanging in there with me and my business."

We stood in the middle of the living room holding each other. I breathed in his familiar end-of-the-day sweat.

"Thanks, Jason," I whispered, eyeing the card stacked with the rest of the mail, shoving aside thoughts of my former life.

Chapter 6—PINK STICK

Jason reached into the dresser drawer late one winter night. "Shit," he said. "The box is empty." I considered searching for my diaphragm in the bathroom closet, but talk about a mood killer.

After my brief stint with the pill in my early twenties, I had opted to prevent pregnancy more naturally and found my way to the diaphragm. I hated most everything about it, from the awkward deployment to the trying search-and-rescue mission hours later. But I'd plodded along with the diaphragm for a decade and then told Jason he'd need to ante up with condoms because I wasn't going to carry the entire birth control load.

"You know," Jason said, turning to face me in bed, empty box still in his hand, "we should talk about commitment."

"You're right," and I pushed my back into his belly so he could spoon me, his steady breath warming the nape of my neck.

Marriage and motherhood had always been part of my plan. I assumed I'd have a house filled with children and would be best friends with other moms. When I was eight, I made my five-year-old brother my baby, swaddled him in blankets, and directed him to sleep and cry on cue. Years later, when the first of my friends delivered her son, she called and told me every detail of the birth, then put her husband on the phone who did the same. I listened again, completely enthralled.

During my final months in Boston, I grieved not only the loss of Brian but also the possibility that motherhood had slipped away. *What if he was my last chance?* I confided to my journal. I don't want to end up "Aunt Kris" for the rest of my life. This is how my friends referred to me in front of their children, a label I grew to resent. Why not just call me "Old Maid," I'd wanted to retort.

Coupling with Jason rekindled my motherhood fantasy, especially when Jason stopped and cooed at every baby he saw. No matter that he didn't know the parents, somehow he'd strike up a conversation, and the next thing I knew he had their baby on his shoulders, all of them beaming. When I saw Jason like this— bighearted, warm, and gregarious—it was easy for me to picture him as a fun and loving dad.

But in our less than a year together, a far-off future with Jason had become hazy, like a humid North Carolina summer afternoon. Was the lust and luster between us wearing off?

I focused on the fun we had. When an ice storm left us without power for days, we played casino and cribbage and back-gammon by candlelight, blankets over our laps and beers in a cooler at our feet. I liked how we always walked hand in hand through town, our interlaced fingers a public statement that we were part-ners and we belonged to each other. We made each other laugh.

It's the small things, I reasoned, that build a lasting relationship.

Then again, I was a northern, liberal urbanite at heart who needed stability and was ready to be settled. Jason was a country-loving southerner, far from settled. He walked into our relationship with his tools, debt, and a vague scheme of growing a start-up business without capital or investors. Me? I had stuff to set up our small house, some money, and a mind that relentlessly planned ahead. Jason's didn't. He knew how to live in the moment better than anyone, and I felt dull in comparison. His idea of fun was hosting a marathon bash with piles of people and heaps of whiskey bottles. Not one part of that scene interested me.

Is our common ground large enough to hold us both? I sometimes wondered.

Our differences showed up in typical relationship arenas, like sharing housework, cooking, or shopping. Jason had agreed to take on the dishes since I shopped for our groceries and did all the cooking. However, Jason's version of kitchen duty meant he'd get to the mess *sometime*, maybe after a shower, perhaps after working on his computer, and if it got too late, in the morning.

"I'll do these later," Jason often said as he'd deposit his dishes in the sink and leave the kitchen.

And I'd sigh. "That's what you said last night."

"I'll do them," he'd say, his voice strained. "But not now. Does it matter if they sit until morning?"

I didn't understand his laissez-faire attitude. Cleaning up after a meal had been drilled into me by the time I was tall enough to peer over a kitchen sink. At the end of each and every family dinner, my brothers and I took turns tackling the kitchen until the dishwasher was loaded and running, pots and pans dried and returned to their cabinets, trash emptied, floor swept. And this didn't mean after homework or TV or anything else we might care to do. My father, after mediating enough arguments about who was on kitchen duty, drew up and posted a huge calendar on our refrigerator, each day of an entire year marked with our names and our scheduled evening job plainly laid out for all the world to see.

We never argued again. And as adults, we each adopted maniacal sweeping, straightening, and tidying practices.

Jason wasn't saddled with this problem.

"Shit. I wish you didn't nag," he often said during one of our regular rounds of messy kitchen distress.

I hated these conversations and remembered the ease of living alone with only my own clutter to manage. Maybe I was just annoyingly picky. But damn it all, I wanted Jason to follow through and own one domestic job. He was so removed from the day-to-day grind of keeping our house picked up, the kitchen stocked, and the bills paid that I began to feel like a housewife. Except that I worked all day in an office.

"Well, Jason," I'd sometimes retort, cringing at how snotty I knew I'd sound, "I wish I didn't need to remind you of everything."

"You know," he'd say, "that sounds like my ex-wife."

And we'd look at each other in dismay. Had we become a cliché already, a couple arguing about chores and money?

~·~

Lying beside Jason, I glanced at the empty condom box. Did Jason and I have enough for the long haul? Did we need more time to settle and gel?

So the best Jason and I came up with in that empty-condom box, god-I-can't-bear-battling-a-diaphragm night was to simply relax because I knew my cycle, and I wasn't in a fertile zone. Besides, we agreed that at our age, getting pregnant probably took more effort and time than one evening romp, if it happened at all. I'd watched friends brave expensive and invasive fertility treatments in heart-wrenching attempts to conceive. Why should I be any more able? So Jason and I forged ahead, both giddy and uneasy with this newfound freedom, as if we were school kids about to get caught breaking the rules.

Strangely and naïvely, that night and in the weeks that followed, even after replenishing our condom supply, we occasionally went without because it was so much easier and so much better. Our periodic unprotected sex, timed to generally avoid ovulation, wasn't an act of trying to get pregnant, we justified, but more like a prelude for when and if we were going to attempt in earnest. A couple of months into our foray of intermittent birth control, my period didn't show up on day twenty-seven of my cycle as it had faithfully since age thirteen. And then it didn't show up on day twenty-eight, thirty, or thirty-two. On day thirty-five, before going to bed, I finally peed on a plastic stick and stared in disbelief as it turned pink.

I called Jason into the bathroom. "Holy shit," he said and hugged me. We stood together at the small sink, pregnancy test lying on a tissue in front of us. "Holy shit," he said again, leaning down to look through the window one more time. He kissed and squeezed me, and we smiled at each other in the mirror. Jason picked up the stick and brought it under the bathroom light. The pink plus sign was still there. "I just can't believe it," he said.

Nor could I. This wasn't supposed to happen so fast. My mind spun. *A baby. I'm pregnant.* Pride percolated beneath my smile. I was fertile; my body worked. On the other hand, I wanted to hit the pause button. "Wait." I wished I could urge the clump of cells multiplying in my uterus. "Just give us a little more time."

We wrapped the stick in the tissue and put it back in the box—our first memento—and climbed into bed. We lay together hand in hand, and I was surprised by an urge to cry.

"What's wrong?" Jason whispered when he heard me sniffle. I rolled into the crook of his shoulder and he wrapped his arm around me. "Tell me what's wrong," he asked again.

"Can we manage this?" I asked.

"Of course we can, sweetheart."

"Really? You're not concerned about money?"

Jason reassured me. Money would work itself out, we'd work our bumps out, and we'd love our baby more than anything.

"This little boy or girl will be the most important thing to us," he whispered, stroking my hair and kissing my cheek. "Be happy, Kris. We're lucky."

I kissed Jason back and willed myself to relax. Closing my eyes, I thought about my adored nephew. I thought of friends in Boston still trying to get pregnant. I imagined holding my baby in nine months, a dream fulfilled. *Don't ruin this moment*, I told myself, *not for him, not for you, and not for the life floating deep inside.*

Chapter 7—SYMPTOMS

In my fantasy pregnancy, girlfriends would surround me, take me shopping, bring me ice cream, and paint my toenails when I couldn't reach them anymore. I'd face the world with confidence and certainty. "I'm pregnant!" my glowing face would announce, as if the life growing in my womb was a badge, the obvious result of good fortune and wise preparation. My doting husband would refill my water glass throughout the day to keep me hydrated, make sure I ate enough, and hell, prepare dinner from time to time.

In the pregnancy that was unfolding, I spent much time alone as my first trimester coincided with the start of summer—and twelve weeks of no work in my position as a learning specialist. The friends I had accrued thus far in Chapel Hill were the few women in my department who, unlike me, worked the entire year. We'd occasionally have lunch, after which they'd return to the office and I'd head home. As for Jason, he was neither doting nor my husband, and I didn't feel compelled to marry him yet. Our pregnancy opened up the idea of marriage, though neither of us felt rushed to take action right away. This version of myself—expecting a child and unmarried—was not who I thought I'd ever be. I didn't feel shame or fear of judgment about this, but my own laid-back attitude about my life startled me. Where had my careful, planning self run off to? How was it that I was living in a small southern town with a man who barely scraped an income together? How was it again that I had given up my well-paid teaching job and now watched every dollar I spent? And now I was going to have a baby? What?

My free time allowed me to become a pregnancy expert, and books littered the coffee table: *The Girlfriends' Guide to Pregnancy*, *What to Expect When You're Expecting*, and *Natural Childbirth the Bradley Way*. I vowed to take care of my body and grow a healthy baby, so I stopped drinking coffee and wine, found myself a midwife practice, signed up for a prenatal yoga class, and added fruits and vegetables into every meal. My body at this early stage demanded food and sleep. Each day was a feeding frenzy as my appetite grew out of control: I needed a full, protein-laden breakfast followed by a peanut butter and jelly sandwich midmorning, then a hearty lunch, and midafternoon cheese and crackers before a full dinner. My level of fatigue, even with daily naps, sometimes made brushing my hair too taxing.

Often when I dried off after a shower, I'd stand on a stool in front of the bathroom mirror to look at my pregnant body. At about the ten-week mark, the biggest change was in my breasts. I could barely stuff them into my regular C-cup bras; they oozed out everywhere, giving me cleavage to die for. And in fact, Jason did die for them, staring lustfully as I undressed each night. These orbs were also so tender I had to shield them from the pelting water when showering. As for my belly, it was only slightly protruded, but my once-tiny waist had thickened enough so that zipping up pants wasn't possible. My summer uniform consisted of sports bras, skirts with T-shirts, and sundresses. Friends warned me about the post-baby weight supposedly hard to lose: "Those last ten pounds are a killer," everyone echoed. But getting fat was not a concern, and frankly, I couldn't imagine it as a problem. My lightning-speed metabolism had always kept me slim, and except for the requisite freshman fifteen that padded my small frame in college, my weight had rarely fluctuated since the age of twenty-one. While some women worried about losing their figure, my worries centered around my body working properly so that my baby would be healthy. Nausea brought reassurance that all was progressing, as did the bevy of other odd pregnancy symptoms: acne, gas, and heartburn.

Each day seemed to present me with a reason to cry, which, according to the books, meant my hormones were in full gear. One afternoon I stumbled upon LeVar Burton of *Roots* fame reading a picture book to a bunch of preschoolers on PBS's *Reading Rainbow*. I fell apart at all those sweet, rapt faces looking up at him.

Small irritations and nuisances would also set me off. On a hot July morning, I took everything out of my purse and laid it on the hood of my car in the bank parking lot. "Where the hell are they?" My voice cracked, fingers searching all the pockets of my bag. "How many times this week have I lost my keys?" Tears spilled as I stood in the blazing heat, wanting only to get home and lie down. "Shit," I mumbled and wiped my eyes with a crumpled, dusty tissue unearthed from the bottom of my purse. I threw everything back in my bag, pushed my unwashed hair behind my ears, put on my sunglasses, and walked back into the bank. My keys were on the counter, right where I had stood ten minutes earlier filling out a deposit slip for one of Jason's meager checks. I sighed with relief and frustration. *Why doesn't Jason take care of his own banking?* I seethed on the drive home.

Before becoming pregnant, I'd been uneasy about Jason's unpredictable work life because I simply wanted our bills paid, wanted the familiar freedom of eating out, buying a new book, or going to a movie. But now I was concerned that in the years to come, Jason and I would struggle to support our child. I'd watched friends earning good money struggle to cover expenses to raise their children. I knew I could always return to teaching and earn a higher salary than what the university paid, though it would still be substantially less than what I'd earned in Massachusetts. Jason continued to brim with confidence that his career as a green builder would prosper once he scored another big job like the house he had finished six months earlier. And those small jobs I kept nudging him to take, that he thought beneath him, continued to earn him only a pittance.

You're fine, it will all be fine, I'd reassure myself when I tired of self-pity. You live in this cute house and you're healthy. You're not rich, but it could be much worse. Still, I couldn't ignore the question that kept surfacing: Could I depend on Jason?

———

"I wonder if it's a boy," Jason said as we meandered hand in hand through our neighborhood one hot evening after dinner. The air was thick with humidity and noisy cicadas. Not ten minutes into our walk, a thin layer of sweat covered my forehead and pooled in my armpits. This was my second summer in Chapel Hill, and I still found the heat oppressive. No way would I ever adjust to the climate.

"If it is a boy," Jason continued, "I'm going to build him a little race car bed."

I squirmed, hating everything about the idea, from the gender décor to the notion of a mini NASCAR scene in my home.

"That's a thought," I said. "Or maybe we just keep things simple. Neutral furniture. Uncluttered room."

"Aw, come on. Let's have fun. I'll build a princess bed for a girl. A throne or something."

Even worse, I thought, watching the laces of Jason's Converse sneakers bounce against the pavement with each step.

"I was thinking we could paint the walls of the baby's room green," I said. "Or what if we paint clouds on a pale blue ceiling?"

"Clouds on the ceiling?" Jason looked at me. "That's weird."

"You don't think it's kind of sweet? Peaceful?"

"Cliché if you ask me," Jason said. "Let's be original. A homemade race car bed is cool."

"I hate NASCAR, Jason."

"You've never been."

"Not interested."

"You're not becoming another snooty northerner, are you?"

As if that was a character flaw. My dreams for my child did not include trips to the speedway or a closet filled with pint-sized camouflage hunting gear. I didn't want my child shooting guns and killing things. Any contact he had with animals I hoped would involve nothing more than chasing my cats around the house or capturing lightning bugs in the summer.

"This conversation is silly," I said. "We're a long way off from choosing a bed."

"Yeah, but it's fun to talk about this stuff," Jason retorted, squeezing my hand once before dropping his and sticking it into his pocket. "Or it should be."

The rest of the walk was quiet.

———

Jason joined me for several early appointments with the midwives, and we cried when we heard the baby's heartbeat for the first time. At the steady *whoosh, whoosh, whoosh* playing from the small speaker of the fetal Doppler, I looked up at Jason's gentle eyes and wide grin. He kissed the back of my hand, midwife smiling too. The tangible evidence of life softened us, and we snuggled on the couch in the evenings and perused the baby name book.

But as summer continued, I noticed Jason seemed stuck, more disorganized and scattered than ever. He neglected to return customers' calls, forgot to load necessary tools in his truck, and misplaced important documents in the mountain of papers on his desk. We bickered about money, housework, what to watch on TV.

Since I had the steady job, albeit three-quarter time, I feared that I'd end up as the working parent while he'd be the at-home one. *Why does this bother me so much?* I wondered one night while I lay awake. I loved that both of my brothers co-parented their children, loved the idea of fathers caring for babies. Except for breastfeeding, I believed men could fulfill a baby's needs as well as women, and could be just as loving, tender, intuitive, and patient. Could Jason, the very man I had impulsively coupled up with? His breath was steady and deep, as it was each night. No more than a two-minute transition was needed between when his head sank into his pillow and when sleep carried him away until morning. Damn him. He slept effortlessly. Needed me to stay financially afloat. And now he might end up with the job I wanted? Jason was a lot of things, but reliable didn't top the list. Didn't matter that I was nauseous, weepy, and pregnant; I still managed the housework, the bills, and the cooking and knew I always would. Could Jason manage himself *and* our baby?

Once I admitted to myself that I didn't fully trust Jason to capably parent our unborn child, I may as well have given him a relationship demotion. And as long, hot August days finally gave way to September, my images of our someday family included Jason less. I imagined rushing home from work to relieve Jason from baby duty, pushing a stroller through the neighborhood while Jason picked up forgotten building supplies at Home Depot for an odd weekend carpentry job. I'd nuzzle up with a baby and chunky picture books each night while Jason worked on his never-finished website. And I'd spoon cereal into our hungry toddler's mouth, little legs happily kicking away in the high chair as we smiled and cooed at each other. And of course I'd clean up the mess afterward, pay the bills, and run the whole show.

Chapter 8—NIGHT-LIGHT

⟋⟍⟋⟍

The midwives praised my good health and thriving baby whose heartbeat was always steady and strong. "You're a model patient," they all said. I gained weight on schedule, all blood tests were normal, and once I was well into my second trimester, I felt good. Both Jason and I looked forward to the ultrasound, a chance to take a peek at our child in action. My favorite midwife explained that it would also confirm our due date and pick up on any possible abnormalities in the fetus. "But you're in excellent health, no concerning family history for either you or Jason. I'm not expecting any problems." We had discussed amniocentesis, which I didn't want unless she thought it necessary. "Your decision in the end," she'd said, "but as long as the ultrasound looks good, I'm fine proceeding without."

"Don't tell us the gender," Jason told the technician on ultrasound day as I hoisted myself on the steel table in a hospital examination room. I opened my robe to expose my rounded belly while the technician readied her equipment. Jason stood next to me, eyes fixated on the monitor next to us. "You want a surprise, huh?" the young, energetic nurse asked.

I did want a surprise, even though every cell in my body believed we would have a boy. I never pictured myself as a mother to girls, maybe because I grew up with two brothers, and maybe because as a teacher I enjoyed the most mischievous boys in the class, the ones who made other teachers nuts. I loved male energy, and while I would have been thrilled with a girl, that possibility rarely crossed my mind. Older women reinforced my fantasy. I'd at times get an unsolicited prediction from a friendly senior citizen when shopping for groceries. "I know it's early," she'd say, "but I've been around for a long time, and some things I just know. You're carrying a boy." I'd smile and explain that we wouldn't know the gender until the birth, but my certainty grew that in the years ahead, I'd be strolling the supermarket with a little boy sitting in the front of the cart.

"Wow," Jason said repeatedly as the nurse pointed out our baby's various parts, like the heart, stomach, mouth. "Just look at him, Kris, he's moving his arm."

My child, who besides appearing like every other eighteen-week fetus as seen through a fuzzy ultrasound image, looked adorable, little hand reaching up toward its mouth.

"We *made* that." I smiled at Jason with pride and love.

"Turn your heads," the nurse warned when she aimed the wand back and forth across my belly to the baby's lower half. "Come on," I heard her say as I stared at the wall, "turn a little more so I can see what you've got down there." She pushed the wand harder, and as the machine's *whooshing* noises grew louder, my anxiety rose. *Go easy on my baby*, I wanted to say but didn't, not wanting to be seen as an uptight mother. "Okay," she said, "move your leg, baby. Got it! Safe to turn around." And I rolled my head back, staring one last time at the small arms and legs on the screen in front of me.

The technician smiled. "Everything looks great. You're right on track; due date looks good."

We celebrated the glimpse of our baby with high-fat cheese-burgers at a noisy, crowded diner. I was famished, as always, and we were both giddy.

"What if he's born on Christmas?" Jason asked as we dipped fry after greasy fry into ketchup. The due date was January 2nd, and I had already been hoping this wouldn't be the case. A Christmas birth would mean my poor child would have a lifetime of birthdays lost in the midst of holiday madness. His special day would be divided into the Christmas half and the birthday half, and it already felt like too much to plan for. Funny how in my last pregnant weeks, his birth date did cycle through my rotation of concerns, along with whether my three-month maternity leave would be enough, or how we would ever afford childcare. It never occurred to me to worry about a healthy baby.

"Let's just hope he doesn't arrive early," I said. "Once Thanksgiving hits, we'll sail straight through till New Year's, pack up holiday stuff, and then I'll deliver."

"Deal," Jason said. "We'll just keep you incredibly still starting December 24th. No walking, no moving, no talking, no blinking."

We chuckled, and then Jason reached across the table and grabbed my hand.

"Hey, I love you, you know."

Our eyes locked.

"We're going to make this work, Kris," he continued. "We've got a sweet baby who'll be here soon, and I'll be a great dad. I promise."

"I love you too, Jason."

We finished our lunch, walked down the block to my office building, and kissed good-bye. We seemed like an ordinary pregnant couple, and I felt a tentative sense of hope as I started up my computer and settled at my desk. *We can be a happy family*, I reassured myself. *If Jason's career takes off*, I reasoned, *half of our stress will be gone*. I hoped the baby would draw us closer and perhaps bring out a side to Jason that would take charge and get organized. And perhaps bring out a side to me that fretted less.

We rode the post-ultrasound high for as long as possible, cuddling in bed and imagining the first day home with our new infant.

"We'll give him a grand tour of the house!" Jason said.

"That'll be one quick expedition," I quipped.

Our excitement buoyed us, but before long we slipped back into our adopted roles. Jason was the discombobulated entrepreneur, and I was the worrier, hovering over the checkbook each week trying to keep us in the black.

I hushed up about my anxiety. Who was I going to tell, anyway? I did not yet have a solid circle of friends in Chapel Hill, and while I told my coworkers about the general stress Jason and I felt, I allowed them to chalk it up to expectant parental jitters. And what was I supposed to say to my family and Boston friends? "I know this will come as a shock after my well-planned and careful move to North Carolina with Jason, but I'm kind of nervous about parenting together." So no one knew that I longed to be cared for, wanted an occasional foot rub or a home-cooked meal made by someone else's hands. Occasionally Jason threw a frozen pizza in the oven and then wandered back to his desk, leaving me to take it out and slice it up. He kept forgetting to scoop the cats' litter day after day—a task pregnant women are advised to avoid—so I did the job myself, scrubbing my hands afterward and tamping down resentment.

Despite my growing concerns and loneliness, I communed with the life inside me wholeheartedly. Throughout the still moments of my days, I sent messages to my baby floating in my womb, pictured his hand curled under his chin. *Are you awake in there? Listen to this.* I'd stand at my kitchen sink washing dishes, imagining he heard the water running from the faucet. *Do you hear my keyboard clicking?* I'd wonder as I typed away on my computer at work. Stepping off the city bus that shuttled me from campus back to my neighborhood at the end of the day, I'd waddle up the long gravel road that led to my street. *How do you like this bouncing?* I'd push my feet through the pine needles and wonder how his little ears took to my quickened heartbeat. *Once you're here, we're going to stroll all over the neighborhood. Wait till you see these tall trees with red and yellow leaves sailing to the ground.* I pictured myself a year in the future pushing my toddler along the streets in a hand-me-down stroller, wisps of his fine hair fluttering in the breeze, his chubby fingers grasping the safety bar. These images gave me a surge of love so strong that my tension about Jason and money faded. "Kick again, Little Boy," I whispered when I felt him wiggle around inside me, feeling proud when he did. "I'm going to take good care of you," I told him. "You won't have to worry about a thing."

﹏

With ten weeks to go, I turned thirty-nine.

"Happy birthday, Kris," Jason said as we settled on the sofa after a quiet dinner at my brother's. He handed me a small brown box the size of my hand with a navy bow secured on top. I took off the lid and removed the sheath of cotton to find my gift: a two-inch square, stained-glass rendition of Edvard Munch's *The Scream*. I lifted it out of the box and noticed two prongs and a small light bulb on the backside.

"It's a night-light," Jason said. "I thought you'd like it for the baby's room."

"Wow." I stared at the distraught, alien-like figure with mouth agape, standing on a bridge against an angry, fiery sky. "Thanks. It's nice."

After too much silence, Jason asked, "You said you like art, didn't you?"

"Sure." I avoided his eyes. "Yes, I do."

"What's wrong? You're not happy."

What I didn't say was: The Scream? *Are you kidding?* I forced a smile instead. "I'm fine. This is great. Thanks."

"Go ahead and return it. My feelings won't be hurt."

I looked over at Jason who sat with arms crossed, eyes cold, and jaw tight.

"No, I . . . I like stained glass."

My eyes returned to my gift, and I wondered what had gone through Jason's mind when he chose it. Why would I put a scary face in the baby's room?

"You know, Kristen, you're kinda hard to please," Jason said. "I thought you'd like this. I tried." He pushed himself off the sofa and left.

I didn't want to chase after him to repair the night. I was tired, it was my birthday, and I wanted to be nurtured. And on my last birthday before childbirth, I also wanted a sliver of connection to my life as I'd known it. The more my belly grew, the less anchored I felt. The once familiar landmarks that made me feel like *me*—liberal friends, a northern urban vibe, predictable career path, and self-confidence—had receded into the past. And I would soon be in uncharted territory. I felt like I was on a ferry motoring out across the sea, the shoreline gradually vanishing until nothing was visible but water and sky. A new landscape would eventually emerge, but what on earth would it look like? What did I know about caring for an infant? What would my life with Jason look like in the months ahead? Would we still be managing unsteady finances? In one more year I'd turn forty; would my Boston self be completely extinguished by then?

Alone, I opened the gifts both my parents had each mailed: pajamas, slippers, and a fluffy bathrobe. I wondered if I should apologize to Jason for my lackluster response to the night-light. And then a kick. I rubbed my hand along my hard belly. "Hello, baby," I whispered. "You're awake. Hi." And then a few more kicks. Friends had told me how much they loved feeling their babies move, and now I understood. I was sharing my body, day by day, with this small, tender mystery. Sensing him move was the sweetest connection, the opposite of loneliness.

Chapter 9—PASSWORD

~~~~~~~~

After Thanksgiving, my body seemed to double in size, and I was constantly exhausted. Walking even a short distance winded me, my large, hard belly now pushing up against my lungs. I was in no mood to deal with crowded shopping malls and so suggested to Jason that for Christmas, we buy a few more baby things instead of gifts for each other.

"I'll cook a special meal and we'll spend the day quietly," I offered.

Jason agreed, and I wondered if he thought, as I did, that after my birthday we'd be wise to skip a gift exchange altogether: no disappointment for me, no hurt feelings for him. We never discussed the night-light again, even after I exchanged it for a small beaded necklace.

In the remaining weeks of my pregnancy, the strain between Jason and me softened. Maybe Jason took pity on me when he saw me walk with obvious discomfort. Maybe my belief in him grew when I heard him on the phone night after night trying to round up more work. Or maybe the sight of my utterly pregnant body stunned us both. From the side, I looked as if I'd swallowed a basketball, my breasts resting on top. My hips were wider, thighs thicker, face fuller. Ready or not, we were about to have a baby.

On Christmas morning, Jason and I drank hot cocoa, assembled the bassinet, and opened gifts sent from family. We sat at the kitchen table in the afternoon and played rummy 500, my stomach protruding in front of me so that I couldn't fully pull in my chair. "Come on, reach, reach," Jason teased as I stretched forward to pick a card from the deck. When the baby moved, I grabbed Jason's hand so he could feel it. "He's awake," I said. Jason smiled at the series of thumps. "I think our boy wants me to discard the seven of clubs." And with that, Jason slapped the seven on the table and won the hand.

Later, I sautéed steaks with mushrooms and onions, while scalloped potatoes bubbled in the oven. Jason played solitaire and chatted happily while I cooked. Most meals I cooked in solitude, calling down the hall to Jason when it was ready. I hated this routine, as if I were his mother. But here we were together, and even though I still prepared our dinner, Jason was a part of it by virtue of being in the same room. He looked cute leaning over the array of cards lined up in front of him, his brown plaid shirt a welcome change from his usual sweatshirt, and his hair soft and combed. I smiled when I pictured some evening off in the future, our baby sitting in a high chair next to him, the three of us home together, a family. I stepped around the counter to the kitchen table, spatula still in hand, and kissed Jason on the cheek.

"What's that for?" he asked.

"No reason, just happy."

Over dinner we clinked our glasses and toasted our last Christmas as a twosome. "Here's to us, all three of us," Jason said and swallowed the last of his beer.

January second, my due date, came and went. I was officially late, officially dipping into my three-month maternity leave and hating that it was dwindling. Jason and I had an initial childcare plan after I'd return to work in March, and while it seemed our best and only option, I didn't love it. Though our infant would theoretically need me, the mother, Jason would care for the baby solo during the workweek and pick up weekend jobs to supplement my salary. I'd be the full-time parent during my twelve weeks off in the summer, and come fall semester, we had no idea what we would do.

So with Jason gone each day (he thankfully found steady work helping a carpenter design and build cabinets), I began the first days of my maternity leave padding around the house alone. Except to pick up groceries or visit the midwives for a checkup, I hardly left. Even if I wanted to read another baby book, which I didn't, I couldn't concentrate. I loaded *Lord of the Rings* into the DVD player three times but never stayed awake past the first hour. I cleaned, fantasizing about bringing my child home to a spotless house. I attempted to scrub my bathtub, but because of my girth, I couldn't reach beyond the sides so culled through cabinets instead, throwing out old prescriptions, lotions, and powders. In the kitchen, I took everything out of the fridge, tossed out old or nearly finished condiments, and wiped each shelf down. I did the same to the pantry.

And then I tackled the baby's room. I had accrued tons of infant stuff from three baby showers: one with my family, one with my coworkers, and a virtual shower with my teacher friends back in Boston. They'd sent a huge box of gifts, and I'd opened each one in my living room. Other friends sent me boxes of hand-me-downs. I was overwhelmed by the outpouring of love and baby paraphernalia and sorted it all on the floor: sleepwear, jumpers, undershirts, socks, hats, sweaters, blankets, bedding, pacifiers, nursing pads, diapering supplies, bathing supplies, medical supplies, baby sling, monitor, plastic toys, and two teddy bears. "Holy shit," I whispered, facing the piles and a mild wave of panic. "Am I really ready for this?" I had read dozens of books about infant care but still didn't feel fully prepared. What if he wouldn't stop crying or got sick? I grabbed a teddy bear, held it in my lap, and rested my chin on its head. My eyes fixed on a white-and-green cap a friend had knitted for me. Were babies' heads really that small? I leaned forward, picked up the hat, and held it against my chest. "I love you already, little boy. Please bear with me if I don't know what I'm doing when you get here."

I took to using Jason's computer, as climbing the ladder up to the loft where my desk and computer lived was too much for my heavy body. At his desk, littered with papers, magazines, and bills, was where I kept up with email, perused websites, and tried my hand at designing birth announcements. But I could never sit for too long, couldn't get comfortable in any position, whether sitting, standing, or sleeping. I never seemed to sleep more than an hour or so at a time before I needed to adjust a pillow or get up to pee. My phone rang constantly, and I fielded questions from family and friends. "No change yet," I told them, "except that I'm down to one pair of pants and two sweaters. I'll let you know as soon as I have news." I was tired of lugging my body around, tired of wearing the same clothes again and again, tired of waiting.

I had just hung up the phone with a friend one evening and dropped back down on the sofa when Jason came bounding down the hall and into the living room and stood squarely in front of me.

"What's going on with Sam?" he glared.

"What?"

"I just read your email to him. What's going on?"

"What are you talking about?" I sat taller.

Jason, his face now crimson and eyes narrowed to slits, raised his voice to a yell. "What's going *on*?"

I flinched, never before hearing Jason shout. Sam and I had been college sweethearts and had stayed together through our twenties. When I lived in Boston, he'd occasionally call when traveling through and we sometimes had dinner. Sam, his wife, and children lived in Seattle, and over the years we'd sent each other email updates on major life events—like the one I'd sent to him announcing I was pregnant. Jason knew about Sam, just as he'd known about Brian.

"How could something be going on?" I said, hand on my belly, heart pounding. "And why are you reading my email?"

"You didn't log off my computer." Jason paced in front of me. "And you signed your letter 'Love, Kristen.' Tell me what's happening. *Now.*"

I tried to recall what I'd written to Sam, but I was so distracted by my racing heartbeat and Jason's agitated face that I couldn't force my brain to think clearly. As far as I remembered, my email was newsy, mostly about how much had changed for me in the last few years, and that I was waiting to have my first child. With Jason. The enraged man in front of me.

"Talk to me, Kristen. I want an explanation."

"There's nothing to say," I said, my voice now cracking. Jason eyes looked menacing, like those of an angry, threatened animal. Eyes like this scared me. When I'd bicycle through my neighborhood delivering newspapers as a young girl, I'd dread passing the house with the giant German shepherd. He'd troll his driveway, tracking me closely as I rode by, his eyes wide and ears erect. I'd grip the handlebars and slowly pass, willing my twelve-year-old self to stay steady: no speeding up, no swerving away, and above all else no showing fear. I tried the same strategies with Jason. "I promise," I said carefully, pointing to my belly, "I'm not cheating on you. Look at me."

"You signed your name '*love*'!" he fumed, as if my signature was the most obvious and damning evidence of my betrayal.

"That doesn't mean anything. It doesn't mean what you think. I don't cheat, Jason."

Which was something he couldn't say about himself. A few months after I'd arrived in Chapel Hill, I'd sat with Jason at the kitchen table and listened to his admission of the affair he'd had while married to his ex-wife. He described how a simple flirtatious work relationship had grown into an all-out, ongoing, behind-his-wife's-back liaison. The more he didn't get caught, the greater risks he took until his ex-wife stumbled upon an incriminating email exchange. Their marriage had been irreparably damaged, and Jason remained shamed and guilt-ridden for a long time. He'd cried when he confessed this to me, explained how unhappy he had been in his marriage, and regretted the pain he'd caused everyone. And I'd believed him. But just as when he revealed his level of financial debt, I'd added this detail about Jason's past in the "Poor Judgment" file I'd started on him.

"Do you have something to hide?" His voice was suddenly calm but flat, and he knelt in front of me.

"No." My voice shook.

"Then I want your email password!" he hollered and slammed his hand on the coffee table. "If you're not hiding anything, I want access to your email from now on! Give me your God! Damn! Password!"

I began to sob. If either of us said anymore that night, I don't remember. What I do know is that I never gave Jason my password, I never forgot his paranoid explosion, and I never again looked at him the same.

Chapter 10—STILL

~~~~~

One week past my due date, my birth plan was in order, house clean, and hospital bag packed and waiting patiently in the corner of the bedroom. I had just seen a midwife a few days earlier. "You look great. Everything's great," she'd said, and reassured me that they'd take good care of me during labor and that I'd be in the hospital if the baby needed special care. She smiled while listening to the baby's heartbeat. "Can't wait to meet this one," she said and squeezed my shoulder. Before I left, she reminded me that I might feel cramping in the early stages of labor, and told me to call anytime. "Hopefully we won't have to wait much longer," she'd said, "but if there's no change in a few days, we'll talk about inducing." So much for natural childbirth, I'd thought. My mother reminded me later on the phone that my brothers and I were all late babies, that we had arrived when we were good and ready, and my baby would too.

I waited with nothing at all left to do. Except prevent the delicate threads holding Jason and me together from unraveling. We had reached a fragile truce. He apologized for yelling, and I reassured him that my email to Sam and infrequent contact had meant nothing. No matter how much I wanted to shake the crazy jealousy right out of Jason, he remained threatened by Sam, and I needed him to be my ally; I pledged to tell Jason if and when Sam's name popped up in my inbox.

An uneventful evening passed with the television filling the space between Jason and me. I stretched out on my side, sofa cushion sharing the weight of the baby, legs and hips stuffed into stretchy black pants, extra-large flannel shirt straining to stay buttoned over my tummy. "Damn," I'd say periodically to Jason, "I think the baby's trying to punch his way out of me." Strong *thwacks* rumbled inside me throughout the evening, and I felt like I was carrying not a human but a small kangaroo. Jason smiled.

The next morning I awoke from a desolate nightmare. I had been somewhere alone with the palpable sense of being stripped of family, friends, everything—and the acute isolation I felt pulled me from sleep. I remember my comfort at hearing Jason breathing deeply next to me, comfort at seeing my sheets, the sheer curtains in front of the drafty windows, and the yellow LED lights spelling out the time on my clock radio. *It was only a dream*, I thought, though hints of desperation were laced in my relief, and I wanted proof that the nightmare wasn't real. I asked Jason when he awoke if he loved me. He said yes, of course he did. And then he said that he resented the question, the same one that his ex-wife used to ask. "Just doesn't mean as much to say, 'I love you' when it's on demand." Too tired to explain myself, I turned away, and somehow we started another day with another reason to be disappointed in each other.

I dragged myself to a Saturday matinee that afternoon, my first real outing in the new year. I couldn't stand to be home anymore, and I didn't want to spend the day with Jason. The nightmare still tainted my mood, and I felt alienated out in the cold, overcast world. I wore my winter coat, the one I'd bought at Macy's in Boston four years earlier: quilted black fabric, drawstring waist, and fur-lined collar that on Boston's coldest days I'd zip all the way up around my neck. It was the coat I'd worn in Paris with Brian, and photos show me smiling in front of the Eiffel Tower, hair whipped around by the wind, lips stained with cherry-colored gloss, hands shoved in the coat's pockets. Now it hung open on my too-big body; pulling the zipper all the way over my belly was impossible. I bought a ticket for *21 Grams*, and other than recognizing the cast, I knew nothing about the movie. The lobby was crowded and noisy, but I may as well have been in a bubble, everyone seemed so far away and remote. I squeezed myself into a seat in the dim theater, glad to be in the dark and quiet. In an early scene of the film, the female lead lost her children and husband in a car wreck. Her grief—sometimes wildly thrashing, sometimes catatonic—mesmerized me. I remember rubbing my belly throughout the film, a gesture to my baby. *I'm here; are you?* And I remember a few gentle flutters in my womb when the credits rolled and the lights came on. A fiftyish balding man stared at me as I shuffled up the aisle toward the exit, and I stared right back. *Yes,* I wanted to say, wanted to walk right up to him and get in his face: *I'm about to have a baby, I'm alone, and my partner and I are in trouble.*

I don't remember that night, if Jason and I ate dinner together, if we watched TV, if we talked, if I took note of any baby kicks, but I do remember the next morning. We lay in bed and I told him about the movie, about the ex-convict-turned-Evangelical preacher who drove the truck that crashed into the car that wiped out the family. Jason listened intently and said something derisive about Evangelicals, about Christians, and then cast a wider net of his disdain to anybody on the planet practicing any religion anywhere.

"It's all bullshit," he said, his eyes still puffy from sleep, "all make-believe."

"How can you be so dismissive?"

If I had been in my right mind, I wouldn't have responded, would have gotten out of bed to pour myself a glass of orange juice, which is what I craved first thing in the mornings. But instead I walked openly into a dead-end discussion about religion, because in that moment, bursting at the seams with a baby and a week overdue, I decided I needed to defend people everywhere who had a spiritual practice, even if I didn't yet have one myself. As Jason and I went around and around—"Be respectful," I implored; "Don't be an idiot," he retorted—I remember telling myself to stop, just stop, get out of bed and go to the kitchen. I was thirsty and wanted to give both the baby and me a long, cool drink of sweet orange juice. The baby was most active in the mornings, like me, and while afternoon and evening movements were less predictable, he was always up and about first thing, especially after a shot of sugary juice. So while I lay there, futilely asking Jason to stop offending half of humanity for believing in things he didn't, I quietly took note of my quiet baby. And when the morning argument ended, Jason escaped to the shower and I walked directly to the kitchen to fill myself up with breakfast.

I leaned back against the counter after swallowing the last sip of orange juice, both hands on my tummy. "Good morning," I whispered. "Sorry you had to hear another fight."

I had grown used to the stirring of limbs in my belly and no longer waited to feel for it like I had in the early months. It would be like waiting to feel myself breathe. My baby and I had simply shared my body compatibly, each of us going about our business during our respective days. But on that morning, I waited for my baby to kick. Wanted it, needed it.

I sat at the kitchen table and listened to the sound of the shower down the hall, of the refrigerator humming, and the wind blowing outside. Closing my eyes, I breathed slowly and deeply, counting to ten again and again. "Everything's okay," I said softly,

both to the baby and me. "Give me a little nudge, a poke, a push."
Nothing. I opened the fridge and poured myself another glass of
juice, drank it all at once, and sat at the kitchen table.

Over the months I had worried about practically everything:
bearing the physical pain of labor, breastfeeding, being cooped up
in January and February with an infant. I worried about the kind
of father Jason would be, how I might manage as a single parent
if Jason and I didn't make it, even if I had what it took to parent.
Hell, I'd willingly given up so much when I'd left Boston; could I
be trusted to make a lifetime of good decisions for my child when
the recent ones I'd made for myself were questionable? Amid all the
scenarios I prepared myself for, not once did I question my child's
well-being. I only pictured a beautiful, robust infant growing into
a smart and clever child despite his parents' failings.

But a new worry surfaced as I paced the small kitchen. Was
the baby okay?

I heard the back door open and close, and then watched
Jason pull his truck out of the driveway. Wherever he was going
off to on a Sunday morning, he hadn't bothered telling me, so I
decided to run a bath and soak for a while. With Jason gone, I
could focus only on trying to relax. My brother was across the
street if I needed anything, so I undressed and sank into a not-
too-hot tub. I poked my fingers gently across my belly, rubbed
its sides, and swished my hips back and forth. "Wake up, baby," I
whispered. "Please wake up."

The phone rang, and I immediately heaved myself out of
the tub, threw a towel around my torso, and walked quickly into
my bedroom.

"Kristen." I recognized the voice on the other end. "It's Kathy."

Kathy was the one midwife in the practice who was never
nurturing, all business, and I'd hoped that when I went into labor,
she would not be on call.

"How are you feeling?" she asked. "Because I was reading through your records, and if labor doesn't start in two days, I want to induce."

The midwives and pregnancy books had said the same thing: labor must be induced by the end of the forty-second week. I was forty-one weeks and two days pregnant, alone in my house with a baby who hadn't moved all morning. My body was still wet from the tub, and water trickled down my calves and onto the floor. I held the phone with one hand and the towel with the other.

"I'm actually a little worried." My voice cracked. "I haven't felt the baby today."

"When did you last feel it?"

"Yesterday, last night." I lowered myself to the edge of my bed, let the towel drop around me, and cried quietly.

"Babies are often less active at the very end," Kathy said. "Have a glass of juice."

"I did already."

And then she told me that I should try not to panic, try not to cry. I'm sure she'd seen it all, a middle-aged midwife who'd delivered hundreds of babies in her practice. She'd seen pregnancies, mothers, and labors of all kinds, including those where babies were less active at the very end, too squished to do much as they geared up for their grand entrance. Why should my baby be any different? There she was in her office on a Sunday, reading through my records detailing one benign visit and test after another, calling to check up on me. What must she have thought when she heard me cry? I was a patient who never complained, was always composed, and took good care of myself. I was easy, and doctors and nurses liked me for the same reasons former teachers and employers had: I was perceived as quiet, competent, nondemanding.

But neither my tears nor unmoving baby alarmed Kathy. Would one of the other midwives been alarmed, asked to see me immediately? Would it have mattered?

"What I want you to do," she said, "is call me if nothing changes within two hours. Try your best to relax. You'll be okay."

I wasn't okay, but I managed. What I did was wash dishes, write in my journal, and sit in the rocking chair, all the while monitoring the time and my belly with vigilance, trying to detect even the slightest flutter. I replayed the previous evening, hoping that by remembering the details of the night, I'd remember when I'd felt a kick from the baby. Was it at bedtime, at dinner? Maybe he'd kicked early this morning, before Jason and I argued, and I simply hadn't noticed?

And then a stab of guilt. How could I not notice? What kind of mother was I?

What I didn't do that early afternoon was phone anyone, not my brother right across the street, nor my mother in New York who had been waiting for The Call. I didn't even try to reach Jason on his cell phone. I kept silent—standard operating procedure when afraid. According to family history, I had spent my first days in nursery school as my brother had before me—sitting by the door with my jacket zipped up to my chin, hand on my backpack beside me. Didn't cry, wouldn't speak to the teacher, just sat there waiting for my mother to get me.

I was genetically wired to suck it up.

But when Jason walked in the house shortly before I'd reached the two-hour mark, scowl still on his face, my composure broke apart.

"Something's wrong," I told him. He was at one end of the hall, at the back door hanging up his coat, and I was at the other, by the edge of the living room. "I haven't felt the baby move all day."

In an instant, fear pushed our anger aside, and Jason took charge.

"Let's call the midwife!" he said, alarm in his eyes.

"We already talked," I sputtered through tears, telling Jason about our earlier conversation.

He grabbed his coat and mine. "We're going to the hospital now. I'll call and tell her."

I hurried into the bedroom to get a sweater, and the sight of my suitcase in the corner stopped me. *Do I bring this?* I thought. *Is this the hospital trip?* I stared at the small purple ribbon tied around the handle and pictured everything I had carefully packed weeks earlier: blanket, cap, sleepers and diapers for the baby, and for me a nightgown, sweatpants, and CDs to play during labor.

"Ready?" Jason called from the back door. I put on my sweater, slipped on my clogs, and grabbed my suitcase.

We drove to the hospital through the long shadows cast by the afternoon winter sun. Jason reached over the stick shift and rested his hand on mine and then turned to look at me. His eyes were red, and a deep line was etched between his furrowed brows. He squeezed my hand and opened his mouth as if to speak, but then looked back toward the road. What words could either of us possibly find? We had no choice but to forget the morning fight, forget the last week, and hold on. I closed my eyes while Jason maneuvered the car through lights and pedestrians clustered in the center of town. By the time he pulled into the main hospital entrance, I was counting my breath to ten over and over.

"Go on in," he said. "I'll park and be right there."

I lumbered to the front desk, suitcase in tow, where beaming faces of two elderly women with "Volunteer" buttons pinned to their shirts greeted me.

"Well, hello!" One of them smiled. "Time to meet your baby?"

"Yes," I said, and then told them that my midwife had asked that I go directly to the maternity floor. A month earlier I had gone on the hospital tour, and I knew exactly what to do. Turn left at the volunteer desk and round the corner to take the elevator, the one with the stork painted on the doors.

Chapter 11—TRIAGE

I lay on the examination table in a dimly lit triage room and waited. I'd followed a nurse here, and as soon as she left I'd undressed, put on a thin, blue cotton gown, climbed onto the table, and draped my coat over me. My bag with its small sampling of baby gear tucked inside looked out of place, forlorn, leaning against the empty white wall with my stretchy black pants and sweater neatly folded on top. Packing had taken so long as I'd obsessed about each item to bring, what to dress my baby in for the trip home. Now that I was in the hospital, I wondered if I'd brought enough. Or too much. I felt myself shiver and pulled my coat up to my neck. *I'm healthy*, I told myself, listening to my breath and refusing to cry. *The baby is healthy, and we're both trapped in a dreadful mistake of a day.*

The first to come into the room was a petite nurse whose pink scrubs matched her manicured fingernails. "Baby quiet?" she asked and arranged the stethoscope between her ears and my belly.

"Yeah, pretty quiet."

I searched her brown eyes for reassurance as she smiled and moved the cold end of the stethoscope to a spot on my stomach. Then to another spot. And another.

"I'm not always good at finding a heartbeat," she said, avoiding my eyes. "Let me get a doctor."

She slid out of the room, and it was at this moment that I knew for certain, knew in every tendon, every organ, in every blood cell pumping through my veins that my baby was not well, knew I was about to get terrible news.

I stared at the ceiling unable to move, afraid to adjust even my little toe, as if keeping perfectly still would prevent calamity from finding me. *No* was the only word, the only thought I had, and it took hold of me, echoed in my ears, marched across my tight chest, and seeped out my pores. *No* was so loud, so strong that it stopped me from wondering when Jason might show up, or the midwife for that matter. I was alone on that table in that dark room, lying as still as my baby inside me, trying not to get swallowed whole by the torrent of *no* gushing through me.

The door opened, and a tall doctor came in pushing an ultrasound machine. He said hello. I took note of his frizzy hair and turned away. I didn't want to see what he was doing, didn't want to see his face. I stared at the wall, stared at my bag sitting all by itself, clothes on top, shoes right beside it. The doctor squirted cold gel on my skin and moved the wand across my belly—searching, searching, searching—while noises sputtered from the machine. Finally the wand stopped. I listened to the hum of the machine and all the sounds it made except for the one sound I needed, the one I'd heard with the midwives over and over: the rapid *whoosh-whooshing* of my baby's heart. I waited for the doctor to say it. *Just say it*, I thought. *Just say it and leave me alone.*

"Do you see this?" the doctor asked. His voice was solemn and the words came slowly.

I rolled my head toward him and looked at the monitor. I could never quickly make sense of the sea of grays in ultrasound pictures, but I looked anyway. "This is your baby's heart," he said. "It stopped beating. Your baby died."

I turned my head away. "You can go now," I told him and rolled onto my side, squeezing my eyes shut.

And then almost instantly, the room filled around me. I never saw Jason come in, but he was there first, head next to mine, crying. His skin was cold, car keys still in his hand, coat smelling of frigid winter air.

"I'm sorry," he kept saying. "I'm sorry."

And then Kathy, the midwife, was on the other side of me. "There was nothing you could have done," she whispered in my ear. "I'm so sorry."

My brother showed up next with eyes all red, and when he hugged me, I remember a momentary awareness that it was strange for us to embrace while I wore nothing but a thin gown. And then I heard ringing, someone handed me a phone, and I listened to my mother's voice. "Oh, Kris," she kept saying. All the noise, so much talking and crying, was suffocating.

While the room hummed and whirled, I kept silent, curled on my side. Soon I heard whimpering, soft and gentle and barely audible, as if from off in the distance. My childhood dog made cries like this, cowering in a corner every July 4th, her pathetic whines a little louder with every firecracker burst. My awareness of the whimpers came and went until eventually they drowned out other sounds and filled my ears. Wait. Were these moans coming from me? Yes. But this wasn't crying: no tears, no runny nose, no pained face. This was a groaning—low, steady, and quiet from deep in the gut of my coiled body, and it had a will all its own. And what was this rocking? My knees were bent into my belly and swayed back and forth, sometimes in tandem with the moans, sometimes not. *What am I doing? What's happening? Is this my body? This table is so cold. Why can't I stop moving?* Anxiety kicked in that my mind, the brains behind the operation of everything I understood about myself, might float away and completely sever itself from the flesh and bones balled up on the examination table. I feared I might actually split in two, so I tried to focus. Focus. Lie still. Quiet down. Hold the table.

The midwife's voice cut through the din inside my head.

"When she's ready," she said, "she needs to deliver the baby. Doesn't have to be tonight, but needs to be soon."

Is she talking about me? And then a flicker of clarity. *I'm still pregnant. I'm not exempt from labor and delivery.*

I don't know how long I lay there, but I understood that Jason, my brother, and the midwife were all waiting for me, that I had to move or say something, that they were looking to me to know how to proceed. And in the weeks and months ahead, I realized I had to guide people repeatedly, that despite a hole ripped through the center of my life, most people needed me to take the lead, wobbly-legged and all, because they just didn't know what to make of me, how to talk to me, a woman whose baby had died.

I finally spoke. "I want to go home," I said to Jason. "I need to sleep at home tonight, then I'll come back."

"Here." The midwife handed me a vial each of Ambien and Zoloft. "These will help you tonight and for the next few months."

I dressed, left the robe on the table, and we all rode the elevator down to the lobby. The midwife left first, then my brother. "Try to sleep," they both said and hugged me before leaving the hospital.

Jason and I stood inside for a moment, looked at each other, and leaned our heads against each other. "I'm sorry," he cried again. I couldn't find any words, couldn't find any thoughts, just wanted to escape the blaring lights and noise of the hospital. "I'll get the car," he said, and I watched Jason walk through the doors and into the black night, my bag slung over his shoulder.

After a few minutes I went outside and waited, air so cold I could see my breath, unzipped coat exposing my belly, hands fisted in the pockets. This would fit again in a couple of days. I heard the hospital doors behind me, opening, closing, opening, closing. I heard the familiar whir of Jason's engine when he pulled up. I climbed in, and as we drove home, I heard crying. My crying and nothing else.

Chapter 12—MIDWIFE

~~~~~~

I poured myself a glass of water, drank down a sleeping pill, and sank into the sofa. Even though I hadn't asked for any, I didn't think twice about taking something to knock me out. I wanted to not be conscious, wanted to shield myself from thinking, because if I gave my thoughts airtime, I knew I'd fall into a pit too deep to ever escape. Though I had barely messed with drugs my entire life, I didn't hesitate to take the sleeping pill. I wanted to feel nothing, wanted to close my eyes and vanish.

Forever.

I waited for the pill to pull me under while Jason clasped my hand. He guided my head onto a throw pillow stroked my hair. I kept my eyes closed except for once when we stared at each other. We both apologized. Without actually saying the words—"Sorry our relationship is so fucked up"—we knew that's what the apology meant. We stuck by each other all night and for many to follow. We simply needed each other to survive. It was as if those last toxic fights never happened. I wanted to hold onto him, needed to, and he wanted to take care of me, fully and selflessly.

At last I felt sleepy, closed my eyes and listened to my breath, to Jason's sniffles and soft cries, and felt his periodic kisses on my cheek. "I'm sorry," he whispered many times.

I don't remember how I got into bed, but that's where I woke the next morning. I opened my eyes and for a few seconds felt nothing, remembered nothing. Those were the best seconds of the day. And then the flood of memories. My throat and chest tightened as I rolled onto my side. *Don't think*, I told myself, squeezing my eyes shut, trying to contain myself and ignore images of the hospital room, the ultrasound machine, my forever sleeping baby still in my womb. But they came anyway, accompanied by a rush of sobs.

Jason immediately woke and spooned me, and I pulled his arm even tighter around me, pulling his leg over mine. I wanted his entire body to cover every inch of mine, would have found relief in being completely smothered from toe to head, especially my head. I wanted to somehow plug my brain, slow it down, stop the churning thoughts. But thoughts came anyway.

"I'll never meet my baby," I wept. "I wanted to be a mother."

And when he told me we would try again, that I'd still be a mother, I snapped. "I want to be a mother to this baby. I don't want another."

—❧—

In the twenty-four hours before I returned to the hospital, I divided time between my bed and the sofa, switching locations when I teetered too close to the brink of falling apart, or when fear of the delivery looming ahead made the waves of nausea travel from my stomach up to the edge of my throat. I napped in my bedroom, or tried to until I looked at the cradle in the corner, yellow daisies dotted along the sheets and bumpers. When the refrain of "No, No, No!" at the sight of the awaiting bed became unbearably loud, I resettled on the couch and buried my face in the fur of my cat, who had so sweetly tucked himself under my neck. Jason handled the phone. He spoke in hushed tones to each kind soul who called, and then he choked up and broke down. When the phone rang again, and it did all day, he'd repeat the routine. I couldn't abide watching this Sisyphean-like cycle of torment, so back to the bedroom. During one such retreat, I sank into the rocking chair and gripped the armrests after changing my clothes and pulling my sweats over my belly. My still-pregnant belly.

I played tricks with my mind, forcing myself to imagine that I was stuck in a dream and would soon wake up to my regular life. I might have even bargained, not necessarily with God, but with time. "Please go back a few days. Let me do this again."

By midafternoon, my mother arrived. She got right to work in feeding me: soup, crackers, cheese. I didn't say much to her, not yet anyway, didn't talk much to anyone. But I was relieved she'd found a flight on short notice and felt safer with her in my house, as if she would keep the walls from caving in.

My family stayed all evening, cooking dinner and cleaning up afterward. Jason and I, like invalids on the sofa with a blanket over our legs, accepted this help.

The doorbell rang after dinner.

"I'm Karen." A blonde, middle-aged woman stood in the doorway. "I've just joined the midwife practice."

I remembered hearing that a new midwife was scheduled to start shortly after my due date. I had hoped I would go into labor when my favorite midwife was on call, hadn't wanted to deliver my child with the new one. And yet here she was in my living room, wearing not a white lab coat, but a blue quilted jacket and white mittens.

"I heard your news and I'm so sorry," she said, looking directly at me. "I wanted to introduce myself tonight because I'm on call. I'm going to deliver your baby tomorrow."

"Please sit down," my mother said, motioning to a chair.

Karen sat across from me.

"How are you holding up?" she asked.

I shrugged.

"And you?" She turned toward Jason.

"Okay." He squeezed my hand.

"I want to tell you what to expect tomorrow, if you're ready."

"Sure," I lied, my gut burning, like a rising flame.

And then she explained that as soon as I checked in, she'd give me something to start labor, which could work right away or take hours.

I said nothing.

"We'd also like to take some amniotic fluid from you, see what we can find out."

I hadn't wanted a big needle going anywhere near my baby when amniocentesis was originally offered. Hadn't wanted to take the risk when all blood tests and ultrasounds were normal.

"Why now?" I asked, still hating the idea.

"If there are any genetic abnormalities, better to know now before you attempt another pregnancy. But Kristen, you should know that we rarely find any reason for stillbirths. Some babies just die."

My eyes lowered and I tasted bile in the back of my throat. Jason put his arm around me and pressed his fingers into my shoulder. "We'll get through this," he whispered.

"It's so hard," I heard Karen say, this woman I had known for all of five minutes. "Unfair. I wish I could make this easier for you."

"Can I be knocked out after I check in?" I asked Karen. "I don't want to be awake for any of this."

She paused, the poor thing. That night was the first shift of her new job, and she started it in this house of gloom.

"Well, we can give you a small sedative, but we need to keep you alert. As hard as this is going to be, this is your baby's birth, and you're still the mother. We'd like you to hold him for a while after the delivery. Later, you're going to want to remember."

Jason kissed the top of my head. I couldn't listen anymore. I'd heard enough. I needed her to leave, needed to climb into bed, needed another sleeping pill, needed to vanish. Karen must have sensed this; she stood up and zipped her coat.

"I'm going to let you all get some rest." Karen crossed the room, knelt in front of me, and put her hands on my knees. "I'll see you in the morning."

My mother walked her to the door. I slipped down the hall into the bedroom and wasted no time in swallowing an Ambien. Leaving my clothes in a heap, I crawled into bed and closed my eyes. *Please start working, please put me to sleep.* As I lay in the shadows, I heard Jason let out my family, heard him switch off the lights in the living room, heard him walk down the hall and into the bedroom.

"Kris?" he whispered. "Are you awake?"

I didn't answer.

Chapter 13—Carly

~~~~~~

Jason and I walked slowly and deliberately from the parking deck, across a sky bridge and into the hospital. I must have looked like any other woman about to have a baby: my huge tummy stuck out in front of me, and I had a man carrying my bag and rubbing my back. And I'm sure the fear in my eyes matched other expectant mothers. What set me apart, however, was my lack of urgency. I wasn't doubled over with contractions, wasn't aching for painkillers, wasn't in any rush to check in so I could get the hell off my feet and get on with it.

Like my child inside me, I became still, contained. I had awakened with a racing heart and shallow breath, not at all sure I would survive the day ahead, but my terror didn't leak out in noticeable ways. No weeping, shaking, shouting, or sweating. Fear simply settled into the nooks and corners of my muscles and bones the way it always had, and the only way I could stop it from sucking the very life out from under me was to get small. Pull myself inward, conserve energy, focus.

Karen greeted us and escorted us to our room, and I immediately put on a robe and climbed on the bed. It was ten o'clock.

"You doing okay?" Karen asked, her hand on mine.

"I guess," I answered, surveying the coral-colored curtains, two matching upholstered chairs, and one small sleeper love seat.

"Let's go ahead and give you a shot of Pitocin, which will hopefully get things moving."

But my uterus didn't seem to care about any shot; my body would remain inactive for twelve hours.

As the long day inched forward, Jason never left my side except to eat, something I wasn't allowed to do until after delivery. Whenever he was gone, I watched the door until he returned. It was as if the Jason who raged about my email had never existed. He held my hand continually, refilled my water glass, and offered to fluff up my pillows. I felt utterly vulnerable without him. Nurses checked my vitals from time to time, and the on-call ob-gyn, a woman my age with two solemn students in tow, popped in once to offer condolences, and then again to insert a monstrously long needle into my belly to collect amniotic fluid.

The steady stream of people who visited throughout the day helped me to stay out of the terrifying terrain of my head. My family soldiered on with Jason and me, played cards with us, talked to Karen as she came and went, and retreated to the waiting room when they needed a break. Nearly two years later I would sit in that exact room awaiting my niece's birth. A cascade of tears would flow down my cheeks while I sat among strangers, remembering the long day and night of my own child's birth.

Numbness set in as the hours ticked away. And not due to a sedative, which I had declined. The reason I was in the hospital, the big reason, was overshadowed by the activity of the day. Or at least this is how my brain decided to cope. I didn't, or couldn't, focus on the purpose behind various visitors lending support or medical care: Jason's parents, friends from work, nurses, and the ob-gyn. I didn't fully forget, obviously, that they were there because my baby died, that I was there because my baby died, that

I'd soon deliver my baby who, by the way, died. But I allowed myself—was grateful—to let my mind concentrate only on what was literally in front of me, moment to moment. The floral scent of Jason's mother's hair when she leaned in to hug me. His father's sad-looking eyes as he hovered in the doorway. The bright gerbera daisies on the table, a gift from my coworkers. The gold hoop earrings dangling from the ears of the ob-gyn. The gin rummy hand I played against my brother.

In the early evening everyone cleared out, leaving just Jason and me. We were both tired, I was hungry, and the silence was welcome. Except the rumblings of my fear returned. How could I see and hold my stillborn baby and continue to live? Surely I would die right there on the spot. My body would simply not stand for such an unnatural, blasphemous act, and would expire. And if my body somehow survived, my heart, my soul, my very spirit would not. They'd be forever wounded, and I'd hobble along the rest of my life like a zombie—alive, but not really.

"Jason," I whispered, "I don't think I can do this."

He took my hand to his face and kissed it.

"I'm scared too. But we'll get through. I promise."

"I don't feel a single cramp. Why is this taking so long?" I wondered aloud, and then glancing across the room I eyed what looked like a baby changing station complete with towels, swaddling blankets, and two small caps, one pink and one blue.

"Don't you think they should wheel that thing out of here?" I asked. "We obviously won't be needing it."

"Kris," Jason said slowly. "I think we will be needing that. Or the midwife will after the baby is born."

I stared at him and back at the table.

"She'll probably lay the baby on the table and wrap him up. Or something. Don't you think?"

My mouth was too dry to swallow.

"Maybe we should play a CD?" Jason asked, stroking my forehead.

Why not? Music was part of the plan, the one part that I could still control. So we listened first to Alison Krauss, and then Simon and Garfunkel, and then finally Eva Cassidy. I thought of her bravery as she faced death at age thirty-two, performing right up until her cancer finally stopped her.

As her bell-like voice and soulful ballads filled the room, so did my contractions. Just like that. By the time Jason and I got through the first playing of the Eva Cassidy CD, all I knew was pain. Physical pain for the next four hours. Every contraction seized my body in a twisted jumble of spasms. In between, I held on and waited for the next one. Karen and two nurses managed to come in without my noticing. They surrounded me. Jason was at my head wiping sweat from my brow, and a nurse on each side held a hand. Karen was at the foot doing what midwives do—leading my child out of me and into the world.

And then silence.

I've never been present at the birth of another baby, but I imagine when a living child emerges, the room is filled with cries of happiness and relief, cries from the seconds-old infant, congratulations and laughter. My room was still and hushed. When had the CD stopped playing? I shivered uncontrollably, waiting. At the changing station, three women noiselessly tended my baby, their heads down, their backs to Jason and me. Later it struck me how their silence gave the space a sacred tone.

Karen finally turned toward us, our baby nestled in the crook of her arm, swaddled in an ivory blanket with a pink cap atop her head.

"You had a girl," she said and gently laid her in my arms.

A girl. I almost burst at the surprise. She was a soft, downy cherub with full cheeks and cupid-shaped lips, and was as light as a bundle of feathers. I snuggled her into my chest with an unexpected sense of calm. My baby was finally here, and even though she would not ever make a peep or lift a lid to meet my gaze, she was with me at last. She was perfect—a girl!—and I loved her.

For the next hour or so, Jason and I took turns holding her, he sniffling messages into her ear as tears fell from his eyes. At one point, Karen escorted my family into the room, and the long night showed in their bloodshot eyes. They kissed me, squeezed Jason's arm, and peered at our baby's face. I made sure everyone noted her cupid lips. They also brought me my first food of the day: a package of saltines and a juice box, both of which I devoured in minutes.

Karen was with us throughout our short time with our baby, ensuring that I was tolerating any lingering physical discomfort and giving Jason occasional hugs. Eventually, Karen began to ask necessary questions.

"Do you have a name picked out?" she asked. "We'll need a name for our records. You can always tell us later if you're not yet sure."

Jason and I had been so certain we'd have a boy, that we'd practiced saying Cooper, our intended name, aloud many times. We so rarely practiced with our girl name that when I spoke it, Jason and I looked at each other as if to confirm agreement.

"Carly," I said.

"Carly," Karen said. "Pretty name."

I looked down at my daughter. She was such a little thing and I pulled her in closer. "Carly," I whispered.

Karen then asked us about out wishes for Carly's remains. In the hours between learning of Carly's death and her delivery, I'd only braced myself to endure the pending birth; I hadn't anticipated questions about an autopsy or a funeral, nor had Jason and I discussed options. Yet in that early morning, Jason and I agreed to an autopsy in the spirit of finding answers to Carly's death, though the medical world seemed more interested in answers than I was. *Just leave her alone*, is what I thought but never said. We also decided to forgo a private cremation and formal funeral, and instead would hold a memorial service of our own down the road.

I would replay the hour I spent with my baby in the weeks and months that followed. In my initial days home, I was grateful to have held her and seen her face, but I ached with regret that I'd never unwrapped her blanket, never saw her hands, toes, belly. And later, when I was back in the world feeling every bit a zombie, I would sit myself down for my first session with a therapist and tell him that I hadn't known what to do, that I'd needed or wanted direction and advice from the midwife. Should I have done more than just hold her tight? Should I have asked for more time with her? Also, the decision Jason and I made about Carly's remains would weigh on me for years and fill me with remorse that we did not have her ashes to look into or to scatter. In our sleep-deprived, emotionally overwrought state, Jason and I could not imagine how to pay the fees Karen quoted us for private funeral homes. But certainly we could have arranged a payment plan, or borrowed money, or figured out a way to hold onto her remains without sinking into debt. Why hadn't we asked for a day to think about our choices before making a decision of such magnitude?

But in our hour with Carly, we were unable to clearly focus on anything beyond the present moment: we'd survived delivery, our baby was finally here, she was beloved, and a surreal goodbye awaited us. My family and Karen stayed with Jason and me in our last moments with Carly. They circled around us while my brother read a Rumi poem about grieving and death, of regeneration and God's mysterious love. My eyes stayed locked on Carly's face while he read. I committed her face to memory, or tried to, because I knew the next step was to hand her to Karen.

"Are you ready?" she asked.

I leaned my head near Carly's and kissed her silky cheek, breathed her in, and drew her body into mine. *I'm your mother, I'm your mother, I'm your mother.* I sensed everyone's eyes on me and felt suddenly self-conscious, so I tucked my face even closer to hers. *I'll love you forever and I hope someday we'll find our way to each other again.*

"I'm ready," I murmured into the silence. I soaked in every last image of my daughter and then lifted her away from my chest and into Karen's waiting arms.

Surely the universe paused, or should have, as my time with Carly ended. Surely not a single cloud drifted across the sky, nor did one wave roll atop an ocean.

"You did great," Karen whispered to Jason and me as she looked down at Carly with soft eyes. Karen moved toward the door and paused to smile at me one last time, allowing me one last look at Carly sweetly tucked in her arm. Karen then left the room, Jason grabbed my hand, and I closed my eyes.

Chapter 14—NUMB

"You need anything before I leave you two alone?" a soft-spoken nurse asked before ending her shift. Everyone else had gone, but she seemed reluctant to go.

"I don't think so. I just want to pass out."

"Of course you do." She stood next to my bed with her hand draped on the railing. "This was quite a day. Probably one of your worst."

I forced a smile. "Honestly, the last few days have all been the worst."

"I bet."

"Can you tell me something?" I asked.

"Sure, hon." She leaned in.

"I don't know when Carly stopped moving, exactly, but I wish I'd come to the hospital sooner."

"No," she said without pause. "If you're asking me if you could have done anything to save her, the answer is no."

Jason was already nodding off on the love seat, so she lowered her voice.

"You would have had to be in the hospital the very moment her heart stopped in order to have an emergency C-section. And then maybe, maybe Carly would have survived." Her voice trailed off. "Really, by the time you noticed she'd stopped moving, it was already too late."

"I wish this made me feel better," I said.

"I do too," she said, her soft eyes filling up. "She was beautiful."

"Thank you."

"And I know it might not feel like it now," her eyes searched mine, "but you'll always be her mother."

"I guess," I said.

"I mean it. Even though she's gone, you're still a mother, *her* mother."

Except I didn't feel like one.

After the nurse left, I lay perfectly flat on my back, still. I didn't know what to expect from my aching body, so I didn't shift positions, roll over, or sit up. I didn't dare lay my hands on my stomach. My feet had become too hot to stay another moment in their socks, but I didn't maneuver myself to take them off.

"Jason," I called.

No answer. He was out, stony, breathing heavily.

I called his name again, louder, and again.

My feet felt on fire, my throat parched.

Finally I yelled. "*Jason!*"

He stirred, dragged his long body off the love seat, and removed my socks. He went right back to sleep, and I continued to lie like a rock, drifting in and out of consciousness for a few hours.

As soon as the sun began to brighten the room, a new nurse came in and flung open the curtains.

"I'm taking you to a different room," she whispered. Both Jason and I were too exhausted to question why and simply watched in a sleepy stupor as she hurriedly packed us up. Then she wheeled me through the winding halls of maternity, Jason following behind, and led us into the elevator and up to a floor filled with regular sick people.

"I wish you hope and healing," she said after she helped me into my new bed and before quickly leaving.

"Jesus, I'm tired," Jason said, hunched forward in a chair, knees on his thighs, head in his hands.

"Yeah, and I'm starving," I replied, staring numbly at the ceiling.

Eating was my primary thought, as the only nourishment to pass my lips in the last twenty-four hours had been saltine crackers and juice. Apparently no matter the circumstances of my life, I would always have a good appetite. My newest nurse told me that breakfast was no longer available, and I panicked. The headache that had started was only going to get worse, as was the shaking in my hands, clear signs that my blood sugar level was dropping.

"You'll be the first room served at lunch," she promised as she ran her fingers through her thick, auburn ponytail.

"When's that?"

"A couple of hours."

"I can't wait that long."

"I'm sorry, ma'am. I can get you a granola bar from the lounge. Would you like one?"

Her tone sounded agitated, as if my hunger was the last thing she had time for. She shifted her weight to her other hip and waited for my reply.

"Ma'am?"

"I don't *want* a granola bar," I said tersely. "I need a meal. Why can't I have a meal?"

I stared at her and she stared back. Didn't she know that five hours earlier I'd had a baby? A dead baby? Wasn't it on my chart? Shouldn't that count? *Somewhere in this hospital,* I thought, *someone could surely scramble me a couple of eggs and make a piece of toast. Hell, she could do it herself.*

She looked at me and backed out of the room. "I'll see what I can find, ma'am."

Jason walked over to the bed. He looked awful—puffy bags under his eyes, dirty hair, wrinkled sweatshirt.

"Why don't I go find a food court? Or I can leave the hospital altogether and bring you back a sandwich or something."

"Do not leave me alone here," my voice choked. "If I can just eat, I can figure out how to deal with all of this."

In the next few weeks, my kitchen teemed with meals delivered by various friends and neighbors, too much for Jason and me to ever eat on our own. But in the fifteen minutes I had to wait for that nurse to return with a bowl of instant oatmeal and a banana, I felt desperate and angry—lying in an arbitrary hospital room, famished, without my baby.

I idled in that room for half a day with assorted visitors: my family, Jason's parents, the midwife Karen, and a brief visit from Darryl, the grief counselor. Darryl had tapped lightly on the door and, after peering in to see that I was awake, walked directly to the side of my bed.

"I'm Darryl, a counselor here at the hospital. You're probably in shock right now, so I won't stay long." He looked like he was dressed for an evening out: maroon button-down shirt, matching tie, black slacks, and shiny black shoes. "I'll leave this with you." He handed a folder to Jason and rambled on for several minutes about its contents: articles, community resources, and a reading list. He described a support group right in the hospital, counseling, and how he could help with funeral arrangements.

I stared up at him, took in all his words, and said thank you.

"I'm so sorry for your loss." He finally slowed down. "If there's anything you need before your discharge, just call the switchboard and ask for me."

"He seems nice," Jason said after Darryl left. "Should we go to the support group?"

I had no thoughts about my post-hospital life. No sense of a future. I'd go home, and then what? Return to work? Return to my same old life? The only feelings I had as I lay in that hospital room were relief that the birth was over, and sadness that the birth was over.

So the notion of joining a support group had about the same appeal as the notion of grocery shopping. It would be something to do.

"Sure," I answered. "Why not."

⁓◦⁓

Despite my anxiety about seeing and trying out my new body, I had been prone for far too long and needed to move. So during a visitor-free patch in the afternoon, I took a fresh pair of sweatpants and a new T-shirt from my suitcase and went into the bathroom. I hesitated before looking at my post-childbirth face in the mirror; would I still look like me? My eyes were dull and circled with dark shadows, my complexion pasty. I shut out the lights over the vanity and brushed my teeth. Turning away from the mirror, I carefully undressed and pulled on clean sweats. When my hands grazed my belly, I gasped. My hard, round tummy was gone.

"Oh, God," I whispered into the darkness and leaned back against the sink with my eyes squeezed shut. Then I placed the palm of my hand directly on my stomach and let my fingers sink into the soft, fleshy mass. I moved my hand back and forth from one hip to the other, the space between them no longer obstructed. My fingers traveled upward and bumped into the underside of my breasts. For the last three months they'd ceased being their own entities, as they had no choice but to lie on top of my protruded belly. Now they hung free. My hand floated back to my navel and after a few moments, fell to my side.

It's just me, I thought. *I'm alone.*

"You already have your Zoloft at home, right?" Karen said. Late afternoon light slanted in through the blinds. Where had the day gone? "Here's some ibuprofen; the cramping should subside in the next few days, and the bleeding will taper off in a week or so."

She put the bottle next to the folder left by Darryl. I imagined piles of these folders stacked in the closet of a hospital office, pre-assembled and ready for the next set of bereft parents.

Karen stayed a minute longer, a large pink envelope tucked under her arm.

"Last night's nurses took a few pictures of her," she said. "They're in here when you're ready to see them."

She gently placed the envelope on top of the folder.

"Okay," she paused in the doorway, "one of us from the practice will call in a day or two. But of course, get in touch anytime if you have a question."

I had often, in my last pregnant weeks, imagined the drive home from the hospital. I would sit in the back, eyes locked on my infant snuggled into the car seat. My hand would rest on a small, capped head, and I'd probably urge Jason to slow down regardless of his speed. "How you two doing?" Jason would ask, his eyes checking us out from the rearview mirror. "Still sleeping," I'd proudly report. In the short trip home, I'd tell Jason about every sigh, every move, and every eyelash flutter. The energy in the car would bubble with nerves and glee. The drive would deliver the three of us to our new lives.

Jason and I drove home in silence.

My head propped against the back of the seat, I stared at the road in front of me. The setting sun darkened the sky, and the only sound in the car was the fan blowing heat through the vents. Jason kept his hand on my knee, and I kept my hand on his. We pulled into our driveway and stayed in the car with the motor running. Every light in our house seemed to be on, and I could see my family milling about.

"Ready?" Jason asked.

"No."

I didn't want to go inside. I didn't want to cross the threshold into my house empty-handed. Doing so felt like the final surrender of my fate and Carly's. As if the last nine months had been a blip. As if she didn't exist. As if I hadn't just delivered a baby girl and left her behind in that hospital. As if all of this were normal.

My brother opened the back door, his face illuminated under the outside light. He cupped his forehead with his hands and squinted into the darkness looking toward us.

"I guess we can't stay in here forever," I said. "Let's go."

I sat in my house that night surrounded by family, surrounded by food. People feed the grieving; they see that hole and just want to fill it up. The spread covering my kitchen table looked like a celebration: chicken, potatoes, cheese and crackers, bread, salad, pie, cookies. I took a plate of food with me to the sofa and noticed how the room had changed. The baby swing was no longer in the corner, *Goodnight Moon* was no longer in the bookcase, and the baby sling that had hung for weeks near the coat closet was gone.

"Where is everything?" I asked no one in particular.

"In the office," my mother said. "We thought you'd want it away."

I closed my eyes.

Jason and I huddled together on the sofa under a fleece blanket, a quiet buzz filling the house as the night wore on: the clanking of dishes in the kitchen, the ringing and ringing of the telephone, the hushed words that reported the same message: "She's home, she's holding up, I'll send your love." My mother handed me the phone a few times, and I listened to the shaky voices of more family whose words got lost in their tears. When my father called, he said very little, just cried on the other end of the line. I didn't know what to say. Hearing him upset frightened me, as if his weeping was proof that Carly's dying was worse than I had yet to understand.

Despite exhaustion, I delayed retreating to our bedroom. Jason would go with me, of course, but at some point he'd fall asleep and there I'd be. Alone with my thoughts. Alone with the image of my motionless baby with heart-shaped lips lying in my arms. Surely I'd snap in half.

Eventually someone turned on the television. Good, just sit here and watch. The colors and sounds from the TV screen washed over me while my tender, cramping body hid beneath the blanket.

My family finally got up to leave. "We need sleep," they said, hugging us while we hovered at the front door, "but we'll be back in the morning." Jason and I headed down the hall, undressed with the lights out, and climbed into bed.

"How do you feel?" Jason asked, holding my hand under the blankets.

"Empty."

When I heard his breath become heavy, I gingerly rolled toward the bedside table. The LED lights from the clock radio cast a yellowish light on the pink envelope. I caught my breath. *Who put this here?* I fingered the edge and then held the packet against my chest. Her photos were inside, waiting for me to stare at them, to look closely for a detail in her face I might have missed. But I set the envelope back on the table, drew my hand under the blankets, and turned away.

Not now.

Chapter 15—PHOTOS

The first light of morning peeked through the bedroom window. I crept out of bed without disrupting Jason's slumber to find my mother reading a magazine and eating a piece of toast at my kitchen table.

"Did you sleep?" she asked as soon as she saw me, wiping a crumb off her chin.

"I think so. I'm hungry."

She popped a slice of bread in the toaster and turned the heat on under the kettle.

"What do you want to drink?"

A box of Earl Grey tea sat on the counter next to the coffee maker. Would my body be shocked by a jolt of caffeine after months without? I imagined the taste of bergamot on my tongue. I pictured a swirl of milk transforming the inky color of coffee into a creamy shade of caramel, and anticipated the aroma filling my lungs. I could sip coffee or Earl Grey tea this morning and have a glass of wine at dinner. I could put anything I wanted into my body now.

"I don't care," I sighed. "Surprise me."

Crumbs and debris from last night's smorgasbord were scattered across the kitchen floor. I grabbed the broom and swept the kitchen, satisfied with the small mass I piled into the dustpan and emptied into the trash. Broom in hand, I headed to the dining room.

"Why don't you sit down?" my mother said. "You don't have to clean right now."

"I want to."

Sweeping seemed to be an imperative. I couldn't tolerate another minute of dusty and unkempt floors. So while the water boiled, while my bread toasted, while my mother watched, I swept every inch of my house.

After a wordless breakfast of toast and cereal and tea with my mother, I returned to bed.

"Did you sleep?" Jason asked in his groggy morning voice, rolling to his side and draping his arm around me.

"Yeah, sort of. You?"

"Same."

I scooted my back against Jason's stomach so he could hold me. My eyes landed on the pink envelope.

"Let's look at her pictures," I said, reaching for the envelope and sitting up.

"Now?" Jason asked, rubbing his eyes. "Are you sure?"

Seeing her photos became urgent, like I ought to have at least glanced at them already. Like I was neglecting my baby, that somehow she needed me to do this one simple thing and instead I'd slept, eaten, and cleaned the floors.

"Yes."

A copy of her footprints was inside, along with two Polaroids and one large color print. Carly's image filled the print, so I could see that she was dressed in a white short-sleeved gown with pink lace trim. I counted all ten of her fingers.

"Her face is shaped like yours," I said.

Jason sighed, closed his eyes, and covered his face with his hands.

Was he crying? I looked back at the photo. "I wish I'd put the gown on her," I said, imagining Karen and the nurses doing this together, seeing more of my baby than I had. Or ever would.

I slid everything back in the envelope and returned it to the bedside table.

"I've put them away," I whispered, rolled back on my side, and closed my eyes.

Early that afternoon, Jason's parents arrived with his uncle Arthur and his new wife, Alice. I'd dreaded their visit, delaying getting dressed until the last possible minute. Except for Jason's father, whom I found reserved and sweet, I was easily drained by the rest of his boisterous clan.

My mother and I were on the sofa together when Jason's mother, Louise, barreled through the back door.

"Where's Jason at?" she yelled as she clomped her way down the hall. "I need Jason! Where's he at?"

I held my breath before meeting Louise's eyes. She wore her usual thick flannel shirt over a pair of worn, faded, and baggy jeans. Two braids framed her plain face, unadorned with even a hint of gloss on her thin lips. Jason's mother remained a tomboy into midlife.

"Jason's in the shower, Louise," I said. "He'll be out soon."

"Well, I need help getting Alice out of the van. We can't lift her out of her seat."

I'd never met Jason's uncle Arthur, who'd recently married Alice, his fourth wife.

Louise gestured to me. "Can you run outside and help get her out?"

Hidden by my sides, my hands formed small fists.

"No, Louise. I can't."

As if a light bulb went off, Louise remembered. "Oh, that's right. You just had a baby. Rest." She turned around and headed back down the hall.

"Hurry up, son!" she called to Jason as she passed the bathroom. "We need you outside."

My mother patted my knee, and together we rolled our eyes.

Jason soon wandered into the living room, his hair still wet from the shower. I directed him outside, and he returned five minutes later with the rest of his family in tow. Alice, poor Alice, had no idea where she was. I doubt she knew *who* she was. Deep wrinkles lined her sagging skin, and a thin layer of snow-white hair tried in vain to cover her scalp. Her stare was vacant. Both Jason and Uncle Arthur carefully led her frail body through the front door and into the foyer. Uncle Arthur, thirty years her junior, laid a towel on my favorite yellow chair and then placed his bride down upon it, where she sat slumped, silent, eyes downcast, with a slight tremor in her limbs and face. Jason's family filled the remaining seats in my living room. My mother relinquished her spot on the sofa to Jason but perched herself on a stool behind me.

Maybe the group talked about the weather, maybe they talked about hunting, and maybe they talked about Carly. I tuned them out and stared through the window at the bare trees against an overcast sky while my mother's hand, like a life preserver, rested on my shoulder. Occasionally I looked at Alice who, like me, wasn't talking, and wondered how much money she had and if Arthur made his living marrying wealthy widows. Glancing at Jason, I noticed tears spilling down his cheek.

"I'm going to lie down," I said to no one specifically and left. I sank like a stone onto my bed, pulled the covers around my neck, and put a pillow over my head.

Jason checked on me later. "Are you awake?" he whispered into our dimly lit bedroom.

"Yeah. When is everyone leaving?" I was still in bed, petting my cat who'd fallen asleep beside me.

"Soon." He walked around to my side of the bed and picked up the pink envelope. "I want to show my parents her pictures."

"What?" I sat up. "Now?"

"Yeah."

He was already at the door, envelope tucked under his elbow.

"Bring it back when you're done," I said.

"I will."

"No. I mean *right away.*"

"Don't worry." He looked curiously at me before leaving. "I will."

My chest tightened, and a lump engulfed my throat. I did not want Carly's photos out there with Jason's mother and that old, demented woman. I pictured the group passing them around like playing cards, marring them with fingerprints. Maybe Uncle Arthur would hold one while sipping water, and his elbow would bump into the side of the chair, causing his drink to spill on the photo. Maybe Jason would offer to let his parents keep a Polaroid, without even asking me. I remained motionless on my bed, eyes glued to the door, willing Jason to open it. After fifteen minutes of my fruitless lookout, I could no longer bear the photos being out of my sight. The thought of returning to the social circle in my living room was impossible, so I opened the bedroom door a crack.

"Mom, Mom!" I whispered down the hall enough times until she heard me.

"What's the matter?"

"Please bring me the envelope."

"It's fine; Jason put it on the bookshelf. It's safe."

I pictured the pink envelope sitting on top of the shelf as if it were nothing special, like the day's collection of circulars from the mailbox.

"Jesus!" My voice cracked. "He said he'd bring it right back. What's wrong with him? It was the one thing I asked."

My mother left the bedroom and returned moments later. I felt her eyes on me as I reached inside the envelope and counted the photos. They were there. All three of them. I sealed the envelope, set it back on my bedside table, and then rested against the headboard.

"How am I supposed to live with this?" I asked, pulling the blanket around me and crossing my arms. "I don't think I can."

My mother sat beside me. "Jason's out in the driveway saying good-bye to everyone. Why don't you get out of bed and I'll make tea."

I didn't want to leave my bed, yet didn't want to stay. There wasn't anywhere I wanted to be, but I followed my mother into the kitchen. I sat at the table watching the teakettle build up steam until it whistled like a siren and rattled angrily on the stove. This ordinary domestic image made me want to scream. Or wail. But I stewed instead. How dare Jason's family bring Uncle Arthur and his geriatric wife to my house? How dare they touch my pictures of Carly? And how dare Jason forget to bring them back to me? The clock read two. What the hell was I supposed to do with myself for the rest of the day? And tomorrow?

And the day after that?

Chapter 16—COMPANY

~~~~~~◇~~~~~~

For the next week, my house buzzed with people. Every day brought well-wishers. My mother hadn't yet returned to New York, and my brother and sister-in-law stopped by daily. Jason and I were rarely on our own.

Talking with visitors gave me purpose, something to do and focus on. "Hello," I'd hear myself say over and over, feeling my mouth freeze into a smile.

"Thank you for the food," I said to my coworkers, who filled my kitchen with what looked like a Thanksgiving meal.

"Thank you for the books," I said to one of Jason's house-building mates, who dropped off a bag filled with literature about infant death. His baby had died two years earlier and he was ready to pass on his collection.

"Thank you for coming." This I said to my pack of childhood friends who arrived en masse from California, New York, and New England to shop and cook, and like my family, probably wait for me to break down. I knew everyone was ready to rescue me if I plunged into a well of despair, so they watched for signs of my descent. I heard muted conversations when I was in another room, noticed several boxes of tissues strategically placed around the house. But in everyone's company I kept myself together.

My feelings wait for solitude before revealing themselves fully, always first needing a private audience with just me. This has been true since I was a little girl. Once my mother found eleven-year-old me whimpering in bed long after I should have been asleep.

"What is it?" she'd asked, sitting next to me, stroking my hair.

In a few weeks, I was headed off to camp for the summer, my first time away from home.

"I don't want to go," I cried. "It's too far away, and I'll be alone, without my family."

I remember my mother asking me how long I'd been afraid and why I hadn't come to her sooner. I'm sure it had never occurred to me to tiptoe downstairs to my parents' bedroom and ask for help. They would have comforted me, but even at that young age, I needed space to make sense of my feelings, especially with fear center stage. And I also needed them to first be only mine.

One evening Jason went to a movie to give me time with my friends. We spread out in my living room, sprawling across the sofa, leaning on pillows on the floor, bowls in our laps heaped with pasta and meat sauce. Joanne asked if I wanted to talk about the birth.

"Really?" I answered. I assumed nobody would ever ask me this question. "You want to hear?"

"You've heard our stories," they reminded me.

And this was true. Listening to friends' labor and delivery tales over the years had made me eager to join the sisterhood of women who'd endured the travails of pregnancy for their adored baby. I'd withstood all the same work, but my baby was gone; could I still be a member?

So I told my friends about the long wait for labor, the epidural that worked on only half of my body, and how I shook after Carly was born.

"I remember shaking too," Joanne said, and Maggie chimed in about her failed epidurals.

We spoke freely, laughing about our oversized, out-of-control bodies, and how time seemed to stop when labor finally took hold. Years later, I understood the magnitude of the gift my friends gave me. For a short time that day, one of the few times ever, I felt like an ordinary mother sharing the story of her child's birth.

"Did you get to hold her?" Katrina asked after bringing our dishes to the kitchen, "and do you have a picture?"

My chest seized. "Yes and yes," I whispered.

"I'd love to see it," Katrina said, "but only if you want."

I brought the pink envelope out from my bedroom, and my friends and I sat in a circle on the living room floor. One by one they held Carly's pictures and the copy of her footprint, carefully passed each one around, murmuring about her perfect lips and sweet little fingers and adorable toes.

When they returned the pictures to me, I looked into Carly's face. Less than seventy-two hours earlier I'd held her. How could I have shared all those months with this small being, and now she was so utterly gone?

I don't know how long I stared at the photo, but Joanne finally broke the silence. "Are you okay?"

"Yeah." I pulled myself inward, too numb to speak, even to my oldest friends in the world. I would later question if I'd been in shock for the initial days and weeks after Carly's death. Even if I'd wanted to find words and talk, would I have been able to?

I slid the photos back in the envelope. "Thanks for looking at these with me." I smiled and added, "And I'm okay, really."

Am I okay? Do they know I'm sad even though I'm not crying? Years earlier, after my friend's father died, her knees had buckled, and she'd fallen to the floor and bawled when she saw all of us enter her house. I envied her ability to publicly unleash her emotions. But that wasn't me.

"I wish she was here with us." Katrina put her arms around me.

"Me too," I said, leaning into her.

That same night, after my friends returned to their hotel and Jason came home, I noticed droplets of milk trickling from my nipples.

Are you kidding? I jammed squares of toilet paper into my sports bra and readied for bed. The midwife had told me to expect aching while my milk came in and then dried up. She should have said, "Your breasts will hurt like hell." Almost instantly they became rock-hard and sore, and I could lie only on my back. I wished Jason hadn't yet fallen asleep so I could complain about the throbbing. How was this fair? If I didn't get to have a baby, I shouldn't have the pain. Yet, beneath the surface of my indignation was a seed of unspoken pride. At least my body had done something right. And even further below was a sliver of comfort, a thread of a connection to my missing baby.

My mother returned to New York the same day my friends left, just in time for my father and brother Tom to arrive. Tom, the family cut-up, joked about my revolving door of visitors.

"Admit it. We're wearing you down," he said after taking our dirty dinner dishes into the kitchen. "One more person offers to get you something or brings you another meal, you'll crack."

I smiled because I couldn't disagree. I was grateful for the outpouring, yet drained. Like all introverts, I need solo time to refuel. I wanted time for silence and to hide in my bedroom for a while. Maybe I would fall into a dreamless sleep, and wake up still pregnant, these last days erased. I'd settle for lying on my bed to stare at the ceiling. But after all the miles friends and family had traveled to be with me, I kept myself going.

With my mother and friends gone, I was suddenly self-consciousness at being the only female in the house with my achy, leaky postpartum body. I felt as if I were having a long, hard period while my uterus shrank back to its pre-Carly size, and I could bear the cramps easier in the company of women. Once my house was emptied of females, I shared my discomfort with no one, not even Jason.

I recall wanting Jason close during these early days, and was grateful for his hushed and gentle demeanor, a far cry from his mood before Carly died. I wanted him in the shower with me so I wouldn't be alone with my naked body. I watched him devour the steak dinner my father made for us, and thought he probably wished I cooked red meat more often. I collapsed bone-weary into bed when I got home from a walk through the neighborhood with my father and brother—my first foray out of the house—and asked Jason to visit with them while I napped. He obliged. He was sweet and protective of me in those initial days, and we bonded anew, even discussed the idea of marriage again. I remember a fleeting hope that maybe mourning Carly's death would bring us closer, repair the damage.

As my father and I sat together at the kitchen table the day he was due to leave, his eyes welled up. "My life has been so good," he said, reaching for my hand. "This is the hardest thing that has ever happened to me. It's so unfair, honey. I wish I could make this better for you."

I wished I could have sobbed, let my father wrap me in his arms, but instead I told him that I was okay, that I would be okay, and that I loved him for visiting me.

Jason drove my father and brother to the airport, leaving me alone for the first time since the day we learned of Carly's death. For weeks, my house had reverberated with voices and hugs and sobs and the ringing of the phone and the thump of the front door opening and closing. Now it was just the newfound silence and me. I stood at the sliding glass doors and surveyed the landscape. Although I couldn't hear the wind, I could see pine trees swaying behind the thick glass. I brought a glass of water into the bedroom and looked around. Should I lie down? Again? On the rocking chair was a new journal, a gift from one of my friends. *A place to put your feelings when they begin to flow*, was inscribed on the inside cover.

I sat down with a pen and stared at the blank first page for several moments.

Finally, I wrote: *Dear Carly.*

CHAPTER 17—SHELLS

As the shuttle van carried us from the airport to the South Seas Island Resort on Captiva Island, I leaned my head against the window and stared out at the banyan trees, the pelicans, and the pink houses. My father had gifted Jason and me with a trip to a luxury resort in Florida with the goal to get away and start healing. But I'd packed my bag with hesitation. I'd hardly left my house since returning from the hospital a week earlier; how could I venture as far afield as an entirely different state?

We arrived on the sprawling grounds in the late afternoon and checked in to our spacious villa. From our screened-in porch we could see a dozen tennis courts nestled in the live oaks, and just beyond, the ocean.

"Pretty nice," I said to Jason. He thumbed through the visitor's guide in the wicker-filled living room, complete with seashell-filled lamp bases and starfish-themed pillows and throws. Now that I saw where we'd live for the next week, my worry about being far from home eased. I'd be okay.

I sat beside Jason and looked in the glossy brochure featuring photos of happy people playing golf, or swimming in one of the five pools, or getting massages in the spa. There were half a dozen restaurants, miles of beach, and cheerful red trolleys to take these smiling people from one venue to another. This trip must be costing my father a fortune. I doubted I'd ever stay in a place this ritzy again and wasn't even sure I wanted to. Brian had taken me to all-inclusive Caribbean resorts, and while I loved the escape from the Boston winters, I couldn't help but think of myself as a slight misfit nursing a sole piña colada all afternoon while the other guests teetered loudly at the poolside bar for round after round of cocktails. Captiva Island seemed a more refined holiday spot, but even if Jason and I had come here for a regular vacation, a financial impossibility, we likely had little in common with its guests.

"Let's go see the beach," Jason suggested.

We followed a lush path through the tennis courts that opened onto the chilly and windy beach. A balmy, sunny afternoon would have been nice, but it was January after all, Florida or not. The ocean always energized me, and the first moments on any beach delighted my senses: salty air, roaring surf, soft sand between my toes, and the vast expanse of sparkling water. Whether swimming through the waves on a hot summer day or walking the shore wrapped in fleece, I came alive at the beach. With Jason beside me, I removed my sneakers, let the salty spray splash against my ankles, and waited for that familiar feeling. I may as well have been at the mall. I felt nothing. A steely sky bled into the lead-hued water. Fellow tourists bundled up in sweatshirts were stooped along the piles of shells dragged in by the tide, searching for treasures. The wind blew relentlessly, flicking my hair into my eyes and knocking seagulls off their spindly legs. I was tired and wanted my feet inside warm socks.

"It's too cold," I said. "Let's go."

Back at our place, Jason collapsed with eyes closed on the sofa while I unpacked the odd array of books we'd brought: humor

(David Sedaris), home improvement (green building), and self-help (surviving infant death). In the bedroom, I pulled out my journal and wrote a few lines.

> *Where am I? Not home with my baby. I'm on an island in Florida. Two weeks ago I was pregnant, waiting for labor. Now I'm at a resort with a sea-green plastic band around my wrist.*

Jason and I eventually visited the nearby deli, ordered sandwiches for dinner, and brought them back to our villa.

"Want to watch TV?" Jason asked.

No, I thought. I hated the blare of TV, and hated in particular Jason's style of watching, which was to cruise the channels interminably. I'd often complain how he wouldn't commit to one show. Jason always promised he would, as soon as he found something good. He rarely did. But I was not about to have our same old, tired argument at the South Seas Resort.

"Watch anything you want," I said, quickly tuned out, and buried my head in a *USA Today* crossword puzzle.

The next morning, like always, I awoke much earlier than Jason and tiptoed out of the bedroom. From the porch, I noticed vacationers strolling the perfectly manicured sidewalks. Their lean and fit bodies wore tennis and golf apparel: form-fitting colorful jackets, leggings and nylon sweatpants, caps, and unblemished athletic footwear. They held small gym bags and sipped from Styrofoam cups. Coffee. I threw on a sweatshirt and sneakers and grabbed my wallet.

The deli was bustling at seven thirty. After being surrounded by family and friends who had tended to me carefully and cautiously, I liked my newfound anonymity. I perused the menu among strangers as if I were just another wealthy woman vacationing. I wasn't the woman whose baby had died, whose breasts were still leaking milk, or whose hips were still too full to fit into anything but stretchy pants or one pair of too large, shapeless jeans. I wasn't the woman who was supposed to be caring for an infant and whose house was filled with baby gear waiting to be packed up. I wasn't the woman who was ready to end her maternity leave early and return to work because what else was she supposed to do?

Here, I could pretend that my life was intact.

"I'll take a hot buttered bagel"—I smiled openly at the barista as if I didn't have a care in the world—"and a cup of coffee with cream and sugar."

"Coming right up," he said and smiled in return.

It worked. I could blend in, sound normal, stand in line with strangers, and order a cup of coffee.

I relaxed into a wicker chair on our porch with my drink, buoyed by my successful solo jaunt. The ocean's briny aroma wafted through the screen, and I could hear the rhythmic thump of tennis balls on the courts. I read the newspaper, knocked out another crossword puzzle, and started a new knitting project. I felt focused and calm as my needles clicked. *Maybe the worst is over*, I thought. Chapel Hill, the hospital, and the bassinet at home were all far away, and I couldn't connect to any of it. *Everyone is expecting me to be weepy and wounded forever, but I am fine. I'm not so different from women who miscarry, and they aren't crippled by sadness for the rest of their lives. Right?*

So I passed the morning imagining I would go forward with nothing more than occasional melancholy. Later, Jason and I braved the trolley to the pool on the other side of the island. We parked ourselves on bright orange lounge chairs with our books and drinks and sandwiches and settled in for a relaxing afternoon. Not twenty minutes later, a young couple grabbed the cluster of chairs next to ours. I smiled at them while they unloaded their gear, and then continued reading. That's when I heard the peeps.

And the coos. I watched as the woman pulled a pink-faced infant out of a carrier. "Hello, sweetie." She cradled her baby in her arms and adjusted the little thing's pink bow secured to ringlets of blonde hair. "Mama loves you. Yes she does."

The baby gurgled.

My stomach flipped. I looked down. *Fuck, fuck, fuck.*

"I hope we won't bother you." The woman turned to us. "We need to stay on this side of the pool where there's sunshine. Too cold in the shade. But she'll be asleep again in no time." And then she turned back to her baby. "Isn't that right, sweetie? You're my sleepy little girl."

Jason reached his hand for mine, but I ignored him, gripping my book instead and staring at the words splashed on the page. My chest hurt, as if someone had reached into the cavity, grabbed ahold of that fleshy mass of my heart, and squeezed. Every inhale burned.

This would become a regular sensation over the months ahead, a feeling of weights strapped to my chest. Every so often, the pressure would inexplicably lift and I could breathe deeply. A reprieve I would learn to savor.

I turned to Jason.

"I want to leave."

"Now?"

"Yes."

Back in our villa's bedroom, I coiled into a ball. "We shouldn't be at this stupid resort," I sobbed. "We should be home taking care of Carly. I can't do this. I don't want to do this anymore."

Jason folded himself around me while I wept.

The spigot to grief opened; the only sounds in the room were my heaves and howls. Only once did Jason get up, and that was to fetch tissues. I grabbed at them, mopping my face and blowing my nose. Eventually I was overcome with exhaustion, and my eyes and nose stopped leaking. Jason and I lay on our backs in the now dusky, silent room, fingers interlaced.

"You want to get dinner?" Jason whispered.

"Sure."

I switched on the lamp and the room flooded with light.

"Let's go to the good restaurant," Jason suggested, his eyes squinting.

"Oh, God. I look terrible and have nothing nice to wear," I said. "Only those jeans fit. And they suck."

They were hand-me-downs from a friend who'd bought them on the T.J. Maxx clearance rack three years earlier when she was postpartum. No offense to Gloria Vanderbilt, but the high waist and sparkly stitching on the back pockets were not my style. But I wasn't about to buy a bunch of new clothes while waiting for my body to shrink, so the outdated jeans were my mainstay.

"It's okay, Kris," Jason said, standing in front of the mirror running his fingers through his hair and buttoning a shirt. "This is how your body is right now, and you still have to eat."

I washed my face, brushed my hair, and stared at my reflection in the bathroom mirror. I looked puffy, splotchy, awful. A coat of mascara and a couple dabs of blush made little improvement. Nor did a white blouse tucked into the jeans. Since none of my belts fit around my thickened waist, I threaded a floral scarf through the belt loops and let the two ends fall from a loose knot at my hip.

"You look good," Jason said when I slipped on black sandals.

"Please. Let's just go."

In the crowded bar and grill, Jason and I ate surf and turf amid the chatter and laughter of men in sports coats and women in cocktail dresses. We were still wrung out from the afternoon's emotional deluge and talked little, but we managed to pose as a regular couple for almost the entire evening. Until I noticed the young poolside family across the room, the baby girl in a pink carrier between her admiring parents.

"Shit," I whispered, motioning to them with my eyes.

"Don't look at them," Jason pleaded. "Look at me. I love you."

I breathed deeply, took another bite of my shrimp, and asked Jason to talk.

"Say anything, just distract me."

He rattled on dutifully about nothing I can recall while I stared at my meal. When the waiter came by to clear our table and offer dessert, I cut him off before he had time to pull the small menus from his jacket pocket.

"Just the check." I didn't glance up toward the innocent server, my eyes fixed on the flickering candle.

"Are you sure, Kris?" Jason asked.

"We have excellent apple pie," the waiter added in a sing-song voice, hoping charm would soften my obvious edginess.

"The check, please." My fingers kneaded my thighs. "Thank you."

While Jason zoned out like a robot in front of the television for the rest of the night, I reclined on the bed with my journal.

I guess I can never be around babies again. Maybe Dad should have sent us to an Elderhostel.

Then a message to Carly.

Where are you? I feel empty. Lost. Everyone has been so kind to Jason and me. It helps, sort of. But all the casseroles in the world won't fill the crater in my heart. I'd give anything to replay these last two weeks, with a different ending of course, so that I could hold you and love you.

On the sunniest and warmest day of the trip, Jason and I returned to the beach. It wasn't warm enough to swim, but we could at least wear T-shirts. Jason parked himself on a blanket, closed his eyes, and faced the sun. He had been mute most of the trip, sleeping a lot, scanning the television for the elusive, perfect program worth watching. He never opened any book he'd packed. He never started serious conversations, but neither did I. We were together yet alone.

"Do you want to walk?" I asked.

"No, thanks. But go and find some cool shells."

"Okay. Be back soon."

The shoreline was littered with shells of all kinds. I'd occasionally stop my stroll, crouch down, and rake my fingers through the piles of coquinas, tulip, and olive shells. As soon as I found what I thought was a beauty, I'd find another more shiny or delicate or brightly colored. I spotted a large conch, completely unblemished, that filled the palm of my hand. The hard exterior reminded me of a cappuccino, a creamy taupe with swirls of ivory. The soft interior was glossy and pink, not unlike the shades of lip gloss worn by my former fifth graders. I'd never before considered a gender for shells, but this seemed utterly feminine: tender on the inside, sturdy on the out. *This is for Carly*, I thought, putting it into my pocket.

And with that, the rest of my walk had a purpose: gather shells for Carly. I had nothing in mind with the idea of this collection—at least not yet—but I felt compelled to round up the most beautiful shells I could find. By the time I returned to Jason, my pockets were crammed with kitten paws, scallops, and tiger moons. I might have shown them to him, but I didn't. I packed them in layers of tissue and carried them back to Chapel Hill unscathed. Eventually, they would find a home in a large hatbox I'd start for Carly, filled with other mementos I'd gather through the years. But the perfect conch, my first offering to Carly, lived for a long time on my bedside table, right beside her photo.

Chapter 18—MAGNOLIA

"Lord, thank you for the many gifts you've given us," the minister's baritone voice called out to the motley crowd, "even for those gifts hard to bear."

Four weeks after Carly's death, a small gathering of friends and family joined Jason and me for an informal memorial service. Barbara, the matriarch of the farm where we'd met two years earlier, offered her home for the occasion. Jason and I sat beside each other at the front of her living room while thirty-odd guests surrounded us, some in chairs and others cross-legged on the floor. An end table turned altar held three tulips in a small vase, the ID bracelet Carly wore on her wrist, and a copy of her footprints that I'd placed in a birch frame.

Looking like a lumberjack in his plaid flannel shirt and beard, the minister continued, "We know you have a plan for each of us, Lord. And we know that we can't always understand your plan."

Cold rain splattered against the picture windows overlooking the fields and gardens beyond Barbara's deck. *Does God really have a plan?* I wondered. *If so, he owes me an explanation.*

I breathed deeply, trying to tamp down my nerves. Kind people surrounded me, though I felt close to only a few and had met many of the guests only once or twice. Had I been in Boston, the familiar faces of long-standing friends would have been a comfort, but I hadn't asked anyone to travel down for the nonsectarian Sunday afternoon service. I was grateful to see my coworkers, my mother, and my brother and his family smiling at me, and I smiled in return at Jason's construction friends and the assorted farm residents.

The minister was well known in the community for his political activism, gregarious personality, and rowdy parties. He didn't have a flock or a parish, but had an ordination nonetheless. Jason had met him through his construction contacts and sometimes shared a beer or a joint with him at the end of the workday. I'd met him a few times.

"We are here to support Kristen and Jason as they honor their daughter," the minister said, turned to me, and officially ushered me into my least favorite place: the center of attention. But I knew I wanted to speak, even with all eyes on me.

"Thank you all for coming." I eked out the words, took a deep breath, and looked down at the folded paper lying on my new black wool pants. Determined that I would not wear jeans at my baby's memorial, I'd gone to Old Navy a few days earlier. I'd quickly tried on half a dozen pairs of pants, and then just as quickly paid for three. I'd needed to nap when back home, drained by the loud music and crowds from my thirty-minute shopping spree. And now as I looked down at the paper in my lap, I didn't care what I was wearing. I simply wanted to get through the afternoon. The only sound in the room was the crinkling of the paper as I unfolded it. That and the banging of my heart against my ribs.

"Dear Carly." My voice cracked. I stopped. My mouth was dry as dust, and my chest ached beneath crushing weight. I'd written a letter to Carly and practiced reading it the day before, wondering how I'd contain myself while allowing a roomful of people access to my private world.

"Your time with me was brief," I continued, "but you won't be forgotten. I wanted to be in your life, and you to be in mine. I miss you all the time."

I'd questioned if people would understand how I could miss my stillborn baby. I would never know her in the intimate way mothers usually know their children. But I missed her presence in my body and in my entire being.

"I miss you when I'm cooking. And reading. I miss you when I'm dreaming. I miss you when I'm breathing," I said as my letter to Carly drew to an end. "I suppose all parents miss their children when they grow up and live their own separate lives. You don't stay with us forever; you're not ours to keep. I hope you feel my love wherever you are now. Even though a piece of my heart is gone, it brings me solace knowing that it is with you."

My trembling fingers refolded the paper. Done. The room was silent. After a moment I looked up. Plaintive expressions looked back at me, my boss blew her nose, and my mother dabbed her eyes. I dropped my head and fixed my gaze on my hand, still gripping the paper.

Jason spoke next and read a poem he'd written about Carly. I remember not one line. But by the end he was crying, and I put my hand on his knee while he wiped his eyes and nose, the guests watching, stilled. *What do they think about Jason's open emotions compared to my composure,* I wondered. *Will I go through my life defensive, proving to the world that I indeed mourn Carly's death even if I don't cry in public?*

Next, my brother invited others to speak. Jason and I hooked fingers while the room filled with words of encouragement, hope, and admiration:

"Carly's close to God."

"Your bravery is a testament to her connection to you."

"Your pain will someday be transformed into something beautiful."

The tightness in my stomach and shoulders loosened. Reading my letter was the hard part of the service, and it was over, and despite the unusual collection of people, their care and concern for Jason and me was palpable.

The rain stopped long enough for all of us to traipse through the mud to a huge field. Pine trees rimmed the edge, and a small headstone at the far side marked the remains of a recently deceased farm resident. Everyone formed a circle around Jason and me while Jason placed a magnolia sapling into the earth. I clenched my muscles and hugged my arms around my belly as the biting, damp wind blew through my coat. Jason confidently spread mulch and fertilizer on the young tree we'd purchased from a nursery. Watching him handle the small magnolia, I realized we needed more moments like this, where he was completely and competently in charge. He knew much about gardening: how to prepare soil, how to tend to new plantings. Not me. All I'd done was pick out the tree. I'd wanted something with pink flowers, and adored magnolia's heady, citrusy scent. A few rosy buds had already formed on the branches, and while Jason put the finishing touches on the base of the tree, I bit my lip when the image of the pink cap on Carly's head flashed through my mind.

Back in Barbara's living room, Jason and I mingled with the guests and balanced our plates heaped with food. It felt good to be done with the ceremony, to be a host, to have a predictable line to deliver. "Thank you for coming," I said again and again as I offered more tea, a slice of pie, another cookie.

One of the guests was Hannah, a French woman I'd met when I was eight months pregnant. She had been sitting at a picnic table out on the co-op's front lawn with her six-month-old. Women bond quickly when holding babies, whether those little ones are inside or outside the womb. Hannah and I had talked, and it wasn't long before she'd promised to lend me her food mill and baby food recipes. As we stood together in Barbara's kitchen, I wondered how she'd discovered that Carly died.

"What will you do?" she asked in her thick French accent, tears rolling down her cheeks. "This is so sad. I'm so sad for you."

"I'll be okay," I said, not knowing how else to respond. "Thank you."

"I just can't imagine how hard this must be," Hannah continued. "To come that far, and then . . ."

She threw her arms around me. I hugged her back, listened to her whimper, and then pulled away.

"You're kind," I said. "Thank you for coming."

Much later it occurred to me that women with living children felt my loss in a way I couldn't. They knew what it was like for childbirth to be punctuated with the sounds of infant howls. They knew what it was like to go home with their babies, to feed them, hold them, love them. They knew. I could only imagine what I was missing.

No sooner had I moved away from Hannah when a guest I'd never met stopped me.

"How are you doing, sweetheart?" she asked, and the next thing I knew she reached out, took my face in her hands, and held it in her hands. "I know just how you feel," she said emphatically. I could see the pores on her nose as she stared into my eyes.

Is that right? I wanted to say, bristling with irritation at her presumption and intrusion into my personal space. *Go ahead. Tell me.* I stepped back, mumbled something about the sun finally coming out, and left.

Jason was across the room talking to a friend from my office. I weaved my way through the guests until I was next to him. He pulled me in for a hug and I melted into his familiar chest. I ate up all the office news my coworker shared with us, like how a quirky student had shown up to an appointment wearing a Wonder Woman cape, and how the coffee shop we frequented had added a new line of breakfast sandwiches to the menu. I was relieved to laugh about the everyday and the mundane, and yet also startled that life in my office had continued in my absence.

That life had continued at all.

Back at home after a subdued dinner with my family, I washed the dishes, Jason dried, and we mustered the remains of our energy to talk. We agreed that the service had gone well and that the tree would be beautiful once covered with flowers.

"Your poem was good."

"So was your letter."

"You think it's okay we didn't invite your parents?"

"Yes. That social scene would have been too hard for them."

Kitchen cleaned, I sank into my rocking chair while Jason puttered on his computer. My journal rested on my lap, though I was too tired to write. The weight of the small book, the words on the pages somehow connected Carly to me and was comfort enough.

Rain started up again, and I pulled a blanket over my legs as cold air blew through the drafty window. I rested my head against the rocking chair, closed my eyes, and pictured Carly's tree, slight yet strong, a symbol of hope and love in that vast field.

"Can you see it?" I whispered. "It's yours. Did you see us today, there for you? Can you see me sitting here, missing you?"

CHAPTER 19—PRETENDING

~~~~~~

The memorial service behind us, the stream of sympathy cards slowed to a trickle, as did the phone calls and visits. I had no choice but to reenter my life.

I left my house each day laden with anxiety, dodging triggers that could shred the flimsy bandages hiding my wounds: the diaper aisle at the drugstore, a pregnant woman on the bus, that boutique next to the bus stop with lacy infant clothes displayed in the window.

Head down, keep going.

Mothers and their babies, a demographic I tried to avoid, were seemingly everywhere. Mothers promenaded down streets pushing strollers, perched their babies on their hips in the post office and the dry cleaner, or cuddled them in slings that hung like pageant sashes across their chests. These cozy pairs swarmed through Chapel Hill like a plague of locusts.

I abandoned my first solo trip to the grocery store due to the sheer volume of cars in the parking lot. I couldn't cope with fighting for a space, so I drove home empty-handed and returned the next morning. I walked among strangers through endless aisles of colors, words, and pictures, Muzak booming in the background.

What kind of cereal did I want? Or laundry detergent? Crackers? Paralyzed by the abundance of choices, I stood and stared.

"Stay away from that woman," fellow shoppers probably murmured. "Something's wrong with her. Just look how she won't move."

When I'd paid the cashier, and she'd cheerfully counted out my change, I'd wanted to cry and scream from sheer exhaustion and the insult of it all. Shouldn't there be an alternate universe for mothers like me? How could we pretend to shop, drive through traffic, and fold laundry as if everything was normal?

But pretending is what I learned to do. No matter how tired or vulnerable, I'd steel myself, leave the safety and comfort of my house, and carefully wade in the stream of life.

During one food-shopping excursion, I maneuvered my cart through the produce displays, turned a corner, and found myself face-to-face with a chubby-cheeked baby dangling in a carrier from his mother's chest. My cart almost knocked into the young woman as she reached for apples.

"Oops," I said, "sorry," and steered my cart around her.

She held my gaze, her smile slowly widening. Her expression seemed to say, "I know you from somewhere," but I didn't wait for her to figure it out. I knew exactly who she was, and I shot out of produce and headed straight to frozen foods. Shit. I waited for my heart to slow down. Did she remember me?

Jess had been in my prenatal yoga class. We'd had the same due date and used the same midwife practice. I'd looked forward to seeing her in the postnatal yoga class we'd both talked about joining.

Sequestered in front of ice cream, I imagined what Carly would have looked like at the ten-week mark: fine flaxen hair coming in, hazel eyes rimmed with long lashes? According to the books I'd read, ten weeks could begin a turning point when the initial shock of motherhood would ease. Would Carly and I have been settled into a routine, running errands together like Jess and her baby? The last time I'd seen Jess we were both eight months pregnant, heading in the same direction on the same path. We were going to be friends sharing motherhood's trials and glories. But while she went forward as planned, picking out apples with her baby for the homemade applesauce she would probably make, I had been jettisoned off the path. I was back at work, or at least my body was. I dutifully went to my office each day, met with students, and attended meetings, but if asked to recount the particulars of any day, I could not recall a single detail. At six o'clock, I'd fall immediately onto my bed with keys, bag, and coat beside me in my unlit bedroom.

And now I was hiding in frozen foods.

If I hadn't already half filled a cart, I would have left. Because if Jess saw me again, she would surely remember. We'd have to talk and hug each other. I'd congratulate her, tell her how great she looked, and fawn over her beautiful baby. Then she'd ask about me. Boom! A landmine would explode on our happy little reunion.

Jess, with her perfect baby in her arms and her perfect shiny apples in her cart, did not need or want to hear my sad tale. I didn't want to upset her, didn't want her to know that my life was an obvious mess when hers so obviously was not.

I ignored my shopping list and quickly tossed random groceries into my cart: frozen pizza, frozen peas, frozen waffles. Peering carefully around the corner before slinking to the checkout, I hoped I could conjure up a lie if Jess spotted me: "Carly is with her father," I'd tell her. "Great to see you, but gotta go."

Once home, I lugged the sundry groceries into my kitchen and immediately turned on the radio and all lights in the living area, my latest strategy to counter the perpetual dreary feeling that had occupied my house since Carly's death. I sorted the mail and opened what would be my last sympathy card, though

I didn't know it at the time. "Thinking about you always," my friend Katrina wrote. "Please call anytime. Even in the middle of the night."

Lovely gesture, but I wasn't wired to make late-night, grief-stricken calls. Still, I liked getting the card because it kept Carly tethered to the world, kept her from fading into oblivion. I didn't want her to be forgotten. I knew that in the months and years ahead, Jason and I would be the sole keepers of her memory. And as the pregnant one who'd given birth, I understood that I'd carry a torch for Carly in a way he couldn't. That nobody could. Would I have the fortitude to privately count Carly's birthdays year after year?

Having aborted whatever plans I had for a meal after jetting out of the grocery store, I wondered what to fix for dinner. The fridge was half empty, and I wasn't hungry. Who knew when Jason would get home? I lay on my couch, gazing out the window at the bare silhouetted trees.

I imagined Jess returning home to a husband who had a steady job, who'd hear her car pull in the driveway and go out to kiss her and the baby, grab the groceries, and escort his family into their bright home. I bet Jess had joined a mothers' group, shared coffee and laughter and stories about her baby with other moms. She probably had a promising career conducting cutting-edge research at Duke, and was conflicted about tending to her work when all she wanted was to tend to her child. She and her husband must have spent lively evenings debating how to manage their careers and parenthood. And then tiptoed together to the nursery to check on their cherubic sleeping bundle of love.

What did Jason and I do? After a bland and boring dinner of plain pasta, or chicken cutlets, or turkey sandwiches, we'd play a few rounds of gin rummy or casino before either turning on the television or retreating to separate parts of the house. Our conversations were benign. Sometimes we'd talk about Carly ("I wonder how big she'd be?"), sometimes we talked about his work ("I made a new contact today"), and sometimes we talked about the house ("Maybe we should plant flowers out front"). Not once did we discuss the huge fight we'd had before Carly died.

How did I end up like this? I wondered. The wind chimes jingled softly out on the deck. *Almost forty, and what do I have to show for myself? If I'd never left Boston, I wouldn't be here, wouldn't be earning a paltry salary, and wouldn't spend the rest of my life wondering why my baby's heart stopped beating.*

The autopsy report had arrived two weeks earlier, and I'd collapsed into the couch after reading the words I'd most feared: Cause of Death Unknown. My seemingly healthy baby had simply died. Did my body ultimately fail to keep her safe? Or did she cut her losses at the last minute, deciding she'd be better off somewhere else? Any way I looked at it, Carly's death was yet more evidence of my inadequacy.

I needed something for dinner. I pushed myself up from the sofa and surveyed the scant contents of the fridge. I ran my hand along my still rounded hips and thighs and eyed half a jar of tomato sauce next to a sad-looking bag of carrots.

Jason's truck pulled into the driveway, and I turned the heat under a pot to boil water for spaghetti. One more uninspired meal. And one more pointless evening.

CHAPTER 20—ANGEL

I read in one of my grief books how bereft parents can cultivate nonphysical relationships with their missing children. The connection can continue, was the message, even after a child leaves the material world.

I grabbed hold of this notion and imagined Carly's spirit floating near me, a comfort as I slogged through long days. I'd sit on the orange vinyl bus seat after work staring out the window, and when I'd ring the bell for my stop, I'd imagine Carly's hovering spirit watching me. I thanked the driver as I stepped off, letting Carly see me playing nice with the world, even though I sometimes wanted to scream at people on the bus who laughed and carried on as if life were easy and predictable and fair. Carly would stay with me as I walked home. Daffodils and forsythia were coming to life, tender dogwood buds waited to pop open, and small sparrows chased each other through the trees. I'd stop and take in this early spring vista, hoping Carly could sense life beating around me, even if she couldn't experience it herself.

In the early mornings, choruses of birds sang outside my open window in a way I'd never noticed before. I wondered if Carly was among them. Leaving Jason to sleep, I'd tiptoe out of the bedroom and slip onto our deck where the rising sun speckled the sky with golden clouds. I listened and searched, hoping to feel Carly's presence with certainty. Surely the earnest trills and warbles of birds hidden in the trees meant something? *Aren't birds connected to the spirit world?* I wondered.

I believed that Carly would communicate with me if I just knew how to read her signals. One warm Sunday afternoon, I was lounging on my deck with iced tea and a book while Jason made phone call after phone call in the kitchen, continually on the hunt for work. A hawk perched on a tree branch thirty feet away, statuesque and still. Slowly laying my book down, I glued my attention to her. She'd sometimes turn her head or raise a wing, and I'd sometimes sip my drink or adjust my sunglasses, but mostly we remained stationary, facing each other. I was convinced this hawk was in my yard for a reason, just knew she was watching me, and I grew delighted with each passing moment. "If it's you, Carly," I whispered, "here I am." I imagined my heart beating beneath my ribs as a cluster of minute pulsating stars. I willed them to push through my chest, glide across the yard and up the tree, bathing the hawk in light and warmth. For what seemed an hour, I had no other thought but the hawk; a marching band could have paraded in front of me and I wouldn't have noticed.

Eventually the hawk lifted herself up and off the branch, pumped her wings, soared through the pines, and disappeared. I went directly to my computer and read up on the mystical symbolism of hawks. I smiled when I learned that shamans believe hawks not only remember past lives but also carry messages from spirits. I was sure that Carly, through the hawk, had come to visit me and stayed as long as she could. The ever-present heaviness in my chest loosened, as I believed I'd just spent the afternoon with my child.

As weeks passed, I lived in dual worlds. There was the ordinary one made up of work, chores, and phone calls with family and friends. And there was the spiritual one through which I tried to commune with Carly. I looked for her everywhere. No longer did I mindlessly whack insects with a rolled-up magazine; now I escorted them, little spirits after all, out of my house with a soothing word and cupped hand. I clung to images in my dreams, searched for their meaning. I once dreamt that Carly was a cat rooting through brushwood for something red. What she was looking for was never clear, a source of worry and frustration, but the color red stuck with me. Days later, I trekked over a waist-high pile of branches and leaves heaped on the edge of a neighbor's lawn to fetch a small strand of red ribbon. It was a splash of color in a sea of brown and gray twigs, and I needed it to be mine. The ribbon lived in my car's cupholder, a little amulet that I'd touch at red lights or before leaving the safe interior for the big, wide open world.

No one knew about the inner life I created for myself, including Jason. I kept my secret life with Carly from him, not due to concern about what he'd think, but because I doubted he'd relate. The last time we'd ventured on the topic of religion had landed us in a bitter argument. That had been the day I ceased to feel Carly move. The day we'd discovered she died. Maybe with our baby gone, Jason and I could have tried to reconnect over the subject of spirituality, opening up an intimate new world for us. But I couldn't bear any risky discussions with Jason. I wasn't about to let anything or anyone, not even Jason, interfere with my mission to be with Carly. Besides, these days I needed to be alone with my journal more than ever, and Jason was buried in small construction jobs while doggedly trying to land a big building project. Discussions with a mystical slant had no place in our shared life.

One night after a hand of rummy, I told Jason I was heading out for a walk through the neighborhood.

"You want company?" he asked.

"That's okay. I'll be back soon."

The dusky evening was muggy, and I passed the occasional couple walking a feisty dog, or a gardener watering flowerpots of geraniums, patches of bright begonias, and impatiens. Halfway through my stroll, a large squirrel dangled in a nearby oak. The gray creature hung upside down, all four limbs wrapped around the branch, swinging like a small hammock.

"Don't fall on me," I whispered to the squirrel, making a wide berth as I walked beneath her. Around the corner and one block later—splat! Without warning, a baby squirrel dropped from the sky and landed inches from my tennis shoes. I shrieked with surprise as the poor thing scrambled to her feet and fled through the bushes.

Back home I sank into my plush yellow chair, my heart accelerated. Clearly this must have been an attempt to get my attention. What message was Carly sending?

"How was your walk?" Jason called from down the hall.

I stared up at the ceiling and considered telling him the simple version, that a squirrel had fallen out of a tree and nearly landed on me, and wasn't that funny? As opposed to the version that played out in my head, that in my quest to connect with our dead daughter's spirit, I'd been hoping that maybe I'd find her in an animal, and guess what? A squirrel, a baby squirrel fell to my feet. Wasn't that wonderful?

From my chair I could see soft yellow light coming from Jason's office, could hear his fingers clicking away at his keyboard.

"My walk was fine," I called back.

On a warm April Saturday, I parked myself at a large table at Kinko's to scan photographs for the digital slideshow I'd offered to make for my brother's upcoming wedding. Sorting through and scanning nearly one hundred photos of two extended families was monotonous, so I created a routine to both speed up the process and entertain myself. One at a time, I placed each photo facedown on the scanning bed without looking at it and waited for the beep to alert me when the enlarged image was visible on the adjacent computer screen. The element of surprise was fun, and I plugged along in this manner, quickly and mindlessly moving through photo after photo.

Until one image stopped me.

Rummaging through my bag for lip balm, I had ignored the scanner's beep. When I finally looked up, an angel filled the screen, complete with wings and a halo. She wore a red robe and looked upward as she blew into a golden horn. Gold filled in the space behind her.

What? I stared in confusion. Examining the photo on the scanning bed I saw a large, medieval, ornate altar behind a group of middle-aged tourists who were so distant in the grainy picture I couldn't make out their faces. Nor did I care who they were. I searched until I spotted the angel, one of several small golden icons adorning the sanctum. She was on the very top, small and hardly noticeable.

I looked back at the monitor. Through no action I'd taken, somehow the small angel had been cropped from the photo and enlarged.

My palms became clammy. *My God*, I thought, sitting back in my chair. *It's Carly.* I saved the angel image to a flash drive, packed up the photos, and left.

Back at home in my rocking chair, I pulled out my journal.

*Hi Carly. Did you visit me at Kinko's? Are you okay? Are
you happy? Wherever you are, wherever you go, remember
that I love you. Remember that I still miss you.*

I closed my eyes and pictured the angel. I wanted so badly
to imbue this image with meaning, because I wanted so badly to
know Carly, to feel her, to be with her. Just like with the hawk
and the squirrel and all the birds, I wanted to know in my marrow
that an angel appearing on my computer screen was my daughter
letting me know that she was okay, and that even though she was
gone, somehow we were still together.

On my bed, I lay on my side and wrapped my arms around
my waist. My downy pillow cushioned my head while puffs of
fresh springtime air wafted through the open window. Before long
my breath deepened, and I slipped into a dream-filled slumber.
Images from my childhood appeared: the backyard with the towering maple tree, a long since deceased family dog running around
our big house, my brothers and father laughing in our den.

And then the best part of the dream.

*I searched the house for my mother. Where was she?
Why wouldn't my brothers or my father tell me? She
wasn't in the kitchen, or in the dining room, or in my
father's office. So I climbed the stairs to the second floor
and turned down the hall to my old bedroom. There she
was, bent at the waist peering into a cradle. My mother
smiled at me as I stood at the threshold. I was scared.
But then she reached into the cradle, scooped up a swaddled infant, and laid her in my arms. I gazed into the
watery, gray eyes of this baby, and she stared into mine.
She was my baby. "I wanted to be your mother," I told
her. "You are," she said. I pulled her in closer.*

Chapter 21—Ally

~~~~

The semester ended in early May, and I was launched into my summer break from work. No more putting myself out into the capricious world each morning; I could stay home or leave the house as I pleased. But the three shapeless months daunted me. What *would* I do? The baby loss books I pored through warned that grief worsened at the six-month mark.

So I could expect the worst Independence Day ever? Great.

I tried to structure my days. After coffee each morning, I'd check the tomato plants I'd started, along with the basil, marigolds, and geraniums. When they felt dry, I had a job, a purpose. I filled the watering can, stood over each plant, and watched the steady stream darken the soil. Sometimes I added fertilizer, rotated the pots, and plucked off brown leaves. After plant duty, the days unfolded with no particular order. Sometimes I wrote in my journal, read, took walks before the temperatures soared, or shopped for groceries. Sometimes I talked on the phone to a friend from Boston. Sometimes I felt okay and took pleasure from watching my cats wrestle each other or my nephew build with Legos. Sometimes apathy took hold, and I felt mired in quicksand in a colorless world. Days like that I napped.

One afternoon, I poked around an infant loss support website and found a page where grieving mothers shared stories about their deceased babies and could write directly to one another. I sent a brief note to a woman on the West Coast who had delivered a stillborn son one month after Carly. She wrote back that night. Our stories were similar—a first and healthy pregnancy, our unmoving infants in our arms, the hard reentry back into our lives. We connected immediately and began to email regularly.

I told Jennifer that at the nearly five-month mark of Carly's death, a dull, persistent ache had replaced my initial shock.

> *I agree with you about the numbness wearing off* Jennifer wrote. *I remember in the very beginning a lot of people said that they thought I was doing so well, too well almost. I also remember knowing inside that it was because I didn't really believe it yet . . . I was just going through the motions. Some days now feel harder than when we came home from the hospital—how is that even possible??*

Jennifer's words were a salve. I wrote:

> *I write in a journal regularly: letters to Carly, poems, and general grumblings about the unfairness of it all. Sometimes, though, I open my journal and I can't think of anything to write, I'm so tired, but just having it in my lap is helpful.*

Jennifer replied:

> *I also have a little book. Someone sent it to me with one of the ten thousand sympathy cards we got. I use it for letters*

to Wheeler . . . and many, many times I just sit with it
open, pen in hand because I don't have anything to say
. . . it's just one of the very few ways I can feel "with" him.

Our steady emails offered a break from my aimless days
and my isolation. We compared notes on everything from Mother's Day plans to when to pack away the baby gear and how our
relationships with friends, family, and colleagues were changing.

Jennifer:

The amount of stamina it takes just to concentrate at
work and get anything done is incredible, not to mention the amount of energy it takes to interact with
people all day. Sometimes I can barely make it to my
car in the parking lot before I fall apart.

Jennifer was an introvert like me, in a professional world
like mine that required she be "on" all day with no time for solitude and refueling. I utterly related to her exhaustion from simply
going to work daily. I told her how relieved I was to be on summer
break and how ineffective I'd been all semester:

I couldn't concentrate. When students talked with me,
sometimes out of nowhere I'd picture the pink cap Carly
had on her head, and I'd wonder why I never thought
to take it off. And then I'd "come to" and pretend I'd
been listening.

Our letters amassed and our bond deepened. Instead of
trying to explain to my family or friends that yes, I was functioning, but no, I didn't feel like myself, I shared all of this with

Jennifer, who genuinely understood. Because we both liked writing—journaling for me had become a lifeline—we reached through cyberspace, grabbed hands, and walked together through our strange new worlds.

———✸———

I told Jason about Jennifer. "I'm glad you found someone to talk to," he said. "I've been worried about you."

Worried? That was news to me. Earlier when I'd told him that I couldn't focus at work and grew anxious leaving the house, he'd seemed impatient. "Maybe you shouldn't write in your journal so much," he'd said. "How will you ever feel better?"

Was he right?

Jason became moody. Were his business struggles wearing him down? Was he tiring of living with someone who craved solitude? Some days he'd seem his familiar self: scattered, a bit disorganized, but generally sweet. Days like this we'd play a pleasant game of cards, cuddle in bed, rent a movie, and attempt to generally connect. Other days he'd blow into the house like a tornado.

"My goddamn truck," he'd glare, slamming his keys on the kitchen table. "I need a goddamn reliable truck."

He'd complain about the jerk who drove like an asshole in front of him, the sticky kitchen drawer, and potential clients who were too damn slow returning his calls. He had no large contracts on the horizon but seized onto the possibility of building a house for a couple who had shown slight and fleeting interest in hiring him. He tried to appear confident in dealings with them, but perhaps they saw the hopelessness in his eyes. Desperation is transparent and never a winning strategy; the couple vanished, and Jason despaired.

Was this what grief looked like for him?

Before Carly died, I would have problem solved and figured out how to get his truck fixed, brainstormed marketing strategies with him. But not now. Instead of listening patiently and agreeing with him that no one in Chapel Hill knew how to drive, I said little. I was always vaguely tired, and the last thing I cared about was an old, beaten-down Chevy or green building.

One afternoon, I returned home from an errand and discovered Jason on my computer. His tight lips gave away his bad mood.

"What are you doing?" I asked.

I turned the monitor to face me and saw my email's inbox opened.

"You're reading my mail?"

Jason stood. "I just can't shake the feeling that there's something I don't know."

"What are you talking about? Like what?" My stomach churned.

"That you're writing to your old boyfriend. Or saying things about me to your friends."

Anger gushed from an unknown place inside of me, and I threw my car keys across the room. "What is the matter with you?" I snapped, "Find something real to worry about, and stay the hell off my computer."

As if regaining consciousness after a mental fugue, Jason's eyes softened. "I'm sorry, Kris," he finally whispered. "I'm having a hard time."

Later that night, after the false laughs of sitcoms flowed from our television, after Jason got ready for bed, I logged onto my email and cleaned out my inbox. I stowed personal emails from family and friends in folders embedded in folders. I changed my password and vowed to log out regularly. I didn't care why Jason didn't trust me. I didn't trust him.

Chapter 22—COUNSEL

Jennifer and I had written about seeing a counselor. And my family floated the idea in front of me as well. "Might be helpful to sort through your feelings with a professional," was the general consensus.

In my first session with Victor, he was mostly quiet while I sat on the tan leather love seat and talked and talked.

"I should have held her longer. Or taken her out of her blanket. I never saw her fingers, belly, or feet. Just her face. That's it."

Every so often I'd stop and gaze around Victor's office, each wall covered with photos, paintings, and poems, his desk piled high with books and papers. And I'd also stop to look at him. A slim man with brown hair and eyes, he looked to be no older than sixty. Something about his space and his still demeanor made me say aloud the things I'd only thought or written about.

"Everybody watched me as I held Carly," I continued. "And I hated it, even though it was my own family. I felt self-conscious. And the midwife was right there, watching as well. I felt like I needed her permission to do more than just lie there with Carly in my arms."

"What would you have liked to do?" Victor asked.

"I don't know. Talk to her. Be alone with her. Apologize."

"For what?"

"I don't know. She died. I was supposed to take care of her. I obviously didn't do that very well."

"Could you have saved her?"

"I don't know," I answered softly. "Babies aren't supposed to die."

∗

I returned to Victor the next week, and the week after that. Being with him in those early months—and in the years that followed—helped me move through the seasons of my life with greater ease.

"Your sorrows are your tribute to Carly," Victor once offered after I told him I thought I'd be sad forever. "Honor her with them. Sit with them for as long as you can."

"I try. But it hurts. Will this ever get easier? How am I supposed to live with this pain?"

"With patience and faith. And by taking care of yourself."

I wanted a road map, a prescribed path leading me to peace and acceptance. Patience and faith seemed too nebulous.

I asked Jennifer about her faith in finding a way to live without Wheeler. She replied with a copy of a letter the spiritual leader Ram Dass had written to a couple after the loss of their daughter. He told the parents that something inside them would die as they bore the unbearable, but also assured them that wisdom and compassion could grow from pain.

I was drawn to the letter's message of hope, especially at the end:

Our rational minds can never understand what has happened, but our hearts—if we can keep them open to God—will find their own intuitive way. Your child came through you to do her work on earth, which includes her manner of death. Now her soul is free...

If I could accept that Carly's life was somehow complete, I pondered, I might accept her death. On good days I even tried to be happy for her. "You're free," I'd whisper to her lonely looking image in her photo, and allowed myself moments of peace that she'd left before any part of this world contaminated her. As for me, the letter sowed seeds of hope that I would somehow heal. I held tight to this possibility and vowed that I wouldn't walk away from Carly's death broken.

But walking away, as far as I could tell, was Jason's plan. I considered showing him the letter, but I knew the message and its spiritual overtones would bounce off him like a rubber ball. I hadn't any idea how he understood Carly's death because he rarely talked about her. And I didn't ask.

One night over our regular card game, I told Jason that talking to Victor was helpful, and asked if he'd be willing to see a couples counselor.

"Why?"

"Because our baby died. Because of our ugly fight before she died. Because we've started fighting again."

He looked puzzled.

"Jason, you were reading my email. Again. You haven't forgotten already?"

He started tapping his cards on the table.

"We've been through a lot, don't you think?" I asked. "I read in one of those 'surviving infant loss' books that we haven't even hit the worst of the grief yet. Might be a good idea to get support sooner rather than later."

After several minutes, Jason silently shuffled the cards, exhaled loudly, and laid his hand on mine.

"I guess it can't hurt."

———⁂———

Susan was a soft-spoken middle-aged woman who had filled her office with plants and bird drawings. Her long auburn hair, beaded necklaces, and Birkenstocks evoked a picture of her as a hippy in her youth.

"It hasn't been the same between us since Carly died," Jason started. We sat beside each other on a soft sofa. "She keeps to herself much more."

"It's true," I replied. "It's not the same. I'm different, and so is he."

"How's that?" Susan asked.

"I don't have as much energy anymore. And Jason angers easily."

Jason told Susan that he tired of seeing me sit in the rocking chair with my journal, and thought I should get out of the house more. I told her that I was tired of watching the once sweet and funny Jason become short-tempered.

Susan said men and women grieve differently, and that we needed to attend to our own mourning while supporting and staying connected with each other.

"This is the hardest thing you'll endure as a couple, and it can actually bring you closer."

Jason reached over and squeezed my hand, and I squeezed back. But I knew we had more to overcome than Carly's death. We hadn't told Susan about Jason's raging suspicions about my college boyfriend, or how we had argued bitterly on the very day we'd found out Carly died, or even about Jason's debt. A stillborn baby was topic enough for our first session.

Chapter 23—Packing

~~~~~~

One morning when Jason was out, I grabbed a few large plastic tubs and stood at the threshold of his office, the would-be nursery. The dresser and closet were filled with piles of baby clothes, heaps of spotless toys, and a collection of baby books. Relatives were coming to town for my brother's upcoming wedding, some staying with me, and I wanted everything out of sight. The last thing I needed was family to dissolve into pity and sadness if they stumbled upon a drawer of unspoiled onesies.

Jennifer had urged me to have someone with me when I packed Carly's things—Jason, my mother, my brother—but I didn't want to. My attention would be compromised with company, and I didn't want to worry about anyone's feelings or expectations. Plus, I wanted to commune with Carly, free of interference.

Jason didn't mind that I wanted the job for myself. "I'll lug everything to the attic when you're finished," he'd said.

And then what, I'd wondered. *Would it stay up there forever?*

I'd avoided the office as much as possible since Carly's death, and I wasn't entirely sure how I'd manage packing up the unused effects of Carly's unlived life. But I braced myself.

First, the books. *The Very Hungry Caterpillar*, *Pat the Bunny*, and a couple dozen others neatly lined a shelf, and I laid each one in the bottom of a tub. I moved on to the toys: the small, pudgy teddy bear with a red checkered shirt, the chunky set of plastic blue keys, the soft and squishy foam blocks. I imagined Carly as a six-month-old, precariously seated on her diapered bottom in the middle of the living room, losing her balance as she reached for a red block. "Whoops," I would have said with a reassuring lilt in my voice, setting her upright again. At eighteen months she might have built a crooked block tower and giggled as I pushed it down with a flick of my hand. "Timber!" I'd cry. "More!" she would laugh. "More!" And we would have played this game until I couldn't stand the tedium. I'd have gathered her in my arms, twirled her around, and sung a silly song to distract her from our falling tower routine. I pictured the blocks faded by the time she was three, bits of foam missing from the corners.

"I worried about all the wrong things when pregnant," I whispered as I tossed a *Baby Einstein: Shakespeare's World of Poetry* DVD into the tub and remembered my search for bilingual day care. "Carly," I murmured, "I hope I would have been a wise mother, not a pushy one."

Blankets, sheets, and quilts sat on a closet shelf, easily filling a second container. On top of the stack was the blanket I'd knit in fuzzy and dense yarns of yellow, white, and periwinkle. I pulled it to my lap. The blanket was huge, would have easily fit on a twin bed and kept triplets warm. Why had I bought that much yarn? I remember knitting and knitting, right up until Carly's due date, wanting this to be her favorite blanket, the one she'd snuggle in when needing soothing. "You know what?" I said aloud, rubbing the blanket against my cheek. "I'll keep this for me." I hung it over the rocking chair in my bedroom, imagined wrapping myself in the soft warmth while journaling.

I brought a shopping bag into the bathroom and tackled the drawer. It burst with baby creams, oils, shampoos, and soaps, and one bottle of lavender body wash I had bought in my final pregnant weeks. I remember waddling down the baby aisle of CVS to buy my first box of diapers, and lingering instead in front of baby bath products. I've always been a sucker for lotions of all kinds, my skin covered in freshly scented moisturizer daily. *You'll be here soon,* I'd thought as I inhaled the crisp, floral scent of a lavender body wash that promised to calm a fussy baby at bath time. Cross-legged on my bathroom floor five months later, I breathed in the aroma again. The smell hadn't changed.

Bathroom supplies packed into the shopping bag, I went to my desk. Carly's hospital ID bracelet was in my desk drawer, along with mine, and I kissed them both. Also in the drawer were Carly's ultrasound picture and seashells from the Florida trip. I found a pink ceramic heart-shaped bowl, placed these keepsakes inside, and decided I'd keep the bowl on my bedroom dresser. I also decided I'd find a plain frame to display the copy of her footprints. Piles of sympathy cards were stacked on the side of my desk, along with the pink envelope that held the Polaroids. An unused floral hatbox made a perfect home for these assorted mementos as well as other items like a handmade mobile created by a friend, a diaper, a candle I'd kept lit my first days home from the hospital.

Finally, the clothes. Back in the office, I prepared myself when I opened each drawer: mounds of socks, neatly stacked undershirts, jumpers, T-shirts, sweatpants, fluffy sleepers in an array of pastel colors, a tiny pair of jeans, and a couple of pint-sized sweaters. I knelt in front of the bottom drawer and pulled out a pale yellow fleece sleeper with a duckling appliqué on the chest. I brought it up to my nose and smelled the baby detergent I'd used to wash each and every piece of clothing while pregnant. Back when I'd readied my overnight bag for the hospital, I'd packed this very sleeper, knowing Carly would stay cozy and warm for our January drive home.

Now, I lay on my back, draped the empty sleeper on my belly, and stared at the ceiling, wishing Carly could have felt my arms around her or looked into my eyes at least once before she died.

Please, please, please. Don't let her be alone.

Closing my eyes, I indulged in a favorite daydream: Carly with Wheeler, Jennifer's son. I didn't envision them as cherubic children romping through heaven's lush meadows alongside bunnies and butterflies and puffy clouds. But I did like to imagine that Carly's essence was with Wheeler's and they took care of each other, just as Jennifer and I were doing as we went forward without them.

Rolling to my side, I got back on my knees and emptied each drawer, piling every last article of clothing inside a tub. "Be happy, Carly," I whispered before sealing and dragging it to the hall with the others.

Later that day, I watched Jason's legs disappear into the darkness of the attic as he hoisted the cartons up to their new home, each one landing with a thud on the attic's plywood floor. We hugged for a few wordless moments afterward in front of the hollowed-out office, my breath heavy and sluggish. I needed to get out of the house. For the rest of the afternoon I stayed on the deck, pressing the tomato plant's small green leaves between my fingers and listening to a couple of crows screaming overhead.

CHAPTER 24—PAPER CLIPS

The evening before family was to arrive for my brother's wedding, Jason and I met with our therapist. Jason folded his arms tightly into his chest, the brim of his cap pulled to his brow and his legs crossed away from me. He spelled out a litany of my wrongs while shaking his foot quickly.

"I put paper clips in the kitchen drawer, and she takes them right out again," was one charge. "She's a control freak," was another. And then finally, "She changed the radio without asking."

Jason stared straight ahead.

Susan's eyes were wide and her lips slightly parted. Was that the moment she knew Jason and I were doomed?

"Would you like to respond?" she finally asked me.

"I don't want to argue about paper clips or radio stations," I said after a few beats.

I didn't want to argue with Jason at all because bouncing back was getting harder. We'd get through one squall only to see a foreboding cumulonimbus on the horizon rolling toward us. Jason once hung up on me when I said no to his phone request to make a Home Depot run for him. I nagged him to stop leaving his dirty clothes strewn on the laundry room floor, and when he didn't, I washed only mine and left his piled in the corner. One morning, I'd changed the station on our bedroom's small boom box while we both readied for the day. Jason became furious that I hadn't asked him first and insisted I change it back to his country station. I refused. We glowered at each other. He stormed into the bathroom. I stormed into the kitchen. And like sparring partners in a boxing ring, we kept to opposite sides of the house for the rest of the morning.

"Kris," Susan repeated, nudging me from my unpleasant reverie, "would you like to say anything else?"

The small couch in Susan's office vibrated as Jason jiggled his foot; I suppressed an urge to toss a pillow or a book right at his offending, dirty flip-flop. I felt Susan's eyes on me as I surveyed the bird drawings displayed throughout her office.

"Kris," Susan repeated, "can you say more?"

"Well," I started carefully, "Jason gets angry a lot, and I don't want to deal with it."

"Why doesn't she respond to what I said?" Jason's voice grew louder. "I'm still pissed about the radio."

Without looking, I knew his cheeks would be flushed. *This is bullshit*, I thought. Susan couldn't say anything that would change the likely outcome of the night ahead, or all the nights ahead. I was wasting money and time discussing radio stations and paper clips. In truth, staying connected to whatever part of Carly I could muster was much more important to me than preserving my relationship with Jason. I didn't care that physical intimacy—once an escape we'd retreated to until the shock of Carly's death wore off—was disappearing. Staring at the row of violets on Susan's windowsill, I understood with laser-like clarity that our relationship was perched on a precipice; one gust of wind would send us falling into the abyss. I wanted the session to be over so I could go home and clean the house before guests arrived. Or write in my journal. Or write to Jennifer.

"Jason, yes, I changed the radio station, and no, I didn't check with you first." My voice was short. "And yes, I took paper clips out of the silverware drawer. Guilty. You do have a desk, you know."

Jason uncrossed his legs and faced me. "I'm goddamn tired of how you control everything." Even through clenched teeth, his words boomed around the room. "Every. God. Damn. Thing."

"Whoa," Susan stopped him. "Settle down."

I was glad to have a witness.

"I'm sorry," Jason said, "but she makes me so mad."

"Your relationship is in trouble." Susan frowned. "If you want to save it, you both have serious work to do."

Jason and I didn't dare talk on the ride home. Not a possibility anyway as he sped along, swerving into the other lane to avoid slowing down for too-slow drivers, the skin on his fingers taut as he clenched the gearshift. He pulled into our neighborhood and skidded to a stop in front of our house.

"Go," he said without looking at me.

I climbed out and stepped to the side of the road just in time for Jason to gun the engine and zoom away, wheels screeching as he turned out of sight.

I wasn't upset and didn't care where he'd gone. I put a Beatles CD in the stereo and turned the volume up high while I swept the floors and scrubbed the bathrooms. Singing about blackbirds, broken wings, and learning to fly, I sang along loudly and unapologetically. "No country music tonight, boys," I said to my cats, who eyed me curiously.

The music ended and the house looked clean enough, so I logged onto my computer.

Hi Jennifer, I wrote. *I'm mixed about the weekend ahead. Part of me is excited about seeing the rest of my family, but will I hold up with all the socializing? At least the next bunch of days will be planned. Going to work was hard, but this long stretch of free time is also hard. Is there anywhere I can be?*

I kept the troubles with Jason vague. While Jennifer and I agreed that our relationships were strained, I knew hers was on solid ground compared to mine. Divulging the ugly side of Jason and me wasn't something I wanted to do. My life had become a spectacle, and hadn't everyone seen enough?

I brushed my teeth and got into bed. My body sank into the mattress, and my eyelids strained to stay open. I reached for Carly's photo on the bedside table. The wedding would have been her first introduction to my extended family. They would have doted on her. She would have worn a darling dress, perhaps one with small daisies and pale green buttons on an ivory background. As for me, I'd be Sister of the Groom and New Mom. Not Sister of the Groom Whose Baby Died. At least no one knew that Deteriorating Relationship was also part of my identity.

"Where are you?" I whispered to Carly's image behind the glass. "When will you visit me in a dream again?"

I returned the photo, closed my eyes, and wondered when Jason would be home. I must have dozed off because I jumped when the phone rang.

"It's me," Jason stammered. "I need a ride."

"Where are you?"

"Tyler's," his voice slurred. "I can't drive."

I considered letting Jason find his own way home from the bar. But starting tomorrow, our house would be filled with guests, and we had wedding events all weekend. If I didn't collect Jason, he would log this grievance against me, and I couldn't risk his temper flaring up in front of family.

Still in my pajamas, I gripped the steering wheel, speeding through the pitch black to the middle of town. I didn't want Jason near me, near my family, or at the wedding. Waiting for me at the curb, he swayed like a windblown cypress, and his head bounced against the headrest the entire drive home. Without speaking, I headed directly to the kitchen for a glass of water, and when I returned to the bedroom, he was draped across the bed, stripped down to his boxers, eyes closed.

I stood over him and shook his shoulder.

"Jason."

"Hmm." He opened an eye.

 "I want to sleep alone."

"What?"

"Go sleep in the office."

"Now?"

"Just go."

CHAPTER 25—TRAPPED

Early the next afternoon, I heard gravel crunch on the driveway; my California brother and my sister-in-law emerged from their rented minivan.

"You made it." I smiled as I joined them outside, grateful for friendly faces. "How was the flight?"

Tom and Stacy each hugged me, but Stacy's went on a beat longer than usual. She hadn't seen me since Carly died, and there I was. Without my baby. Still standing.

"I wish I could have come out sooner," she said, "but I'm so glad to finally see you."

And I was glad to see her too, and my brother, and would be glad to see the rest of my clan as they'd trickle in. Still, I sensed armor forming around me. I was once the Sibling Most Likely to be Happily Married with Children, but a dead baby and a shitty relationship would likely change me to Poor Kris. And I railed against Poor Kris. It had been me, not my brothers, who'd walked the straight and narrow path, never veering off to dabble in drugs or to venture across the country in a rickety van on a soul-searching expedition. I'd adopted the role of Conventional; they hadn't. And while I was happy that my brothers had loving partners and adorable kids, I couldn't help but feel a little bit cheated. I could find little to hold onto that was familiar and reassuring, but I'd be damned if I'd be labeled Poor Kris. Being treated differently, or being viewed through a pity lens was an unbearable possibility, as it would separate, condescend, and patronize. So the armor I wore helped me stand tall, smile, and call forth the version of me that was recognizable to my family and me.

"I'm so glad to see you too," I said to Stacy as I leaned against the minivan. "You all look great."

I peered at my niece and nephew still strapped in their car seats. Cole was barely one, and I had met him only once when he was an infant. Tom unbuckled him and lifted him into his arms. My stomach knotted as I took in the pudgy toddler who would have been Carly's playmate.

"Oh, he's precious," I said. He reminded me of Tom as a baby with his blue eyes and blond curls. As I reached my hand toward him, he buried his head in Tom's shoulder. A pang of self-pity and rejection constricted my chest.

"He's shy," Tom said. "Give him time."

"Come inside, everyone," I said, feigning cheer, and grabbed my five-year-old niece's hand.

"Hey, Aunt Kris, where's Jason?" Tatum asked.

"He'll be back in a while," I answered as we lugged suitcases and tote bags into the house.

The truth was I didn't know when Jason would return. He'd awoken with a hangover and skulked around the kitchen waiting for his coffee to brew, eyes bloodshot and blazing. While folding laundry in the living room, I'd watched him cautiously out of the corner of my eye, expecting he'd apologize for the night before.

"Will you please drive me to Tyler's so I can get my truck?" Jason had finally asked.

"Do you want to tell me what happened last night?" I said.

"I'm pissed," Jason said. "I'm just pissed."

No shit, I thought.

"Why?"

"I don't know. Everything. Nothing. Doesn't matter. I'll deal with it."

When I pulled up to Tyler's, Jason had grumbled a barely audible "Thanks," said nothing about when he'd return home, and loped across the parking lot toward his truck. I'd spent the rest of the morning wondering who would show up at the house first: a still-angry Jason or my travel-weary brother.

Tom and Stacy and I chatted about pre-wedding festivities over turkey sandwiches while the kids half-ate through their obvious fatigue. I suggested they all rest after their long day of travel.

"Please let us clean the kitchen first," Tom proposed, but I gave them the green light for a nap, promising pizzas for dinner and a DVD for the kids.

I was glad they were tired because after my late-night retrieval of Jason, I'd wanted to nap myself. But no such luck. Jason's truck rumbled up the driveway as soon as I'd dried the last of the dishes.

Please, I thought, *no drama*.

"I'm starved," Jason announced, tossing his keys on the table and opening the fridge. Without eye contact, he pulled out sandwich fixings.

In the time it took me to understand that Jason had no plan to offer an olive branch, our small house seemed to shrink even more than it already had. After Carly's death, flowers, sympathy cards, and hospital bills had streamed in, stuffing our house with reminders of our loss. And then there were other reminders, like my leaky breasts that went on and on, and the growing distance between Jason and me. Sometimes it seemed that we couldn't escape the sorrow; it came in through the windows and up through the floorboards, crowding every room. I kept yearning for space and often imagined myself in a vast field or on a sprawling lake, believing my mind would empty and my body would relax in wide open, uncluttered expanses. But now, I'd relinquished my bedroom and sanctuary to Tom and his family so they could pile into one large room and have their own bath. Jason and I would share an air mattress in the stifling-hot loft, a small room without a door whose slanted ceilings made it impossible for even my short body to stand up straight. As if anticipating living like a caged bird for the next four days, my body wanted to wilt.

"Where were you?" I asked Jason, who was busily slathering gobs of mayo on bread.

"Lowes."

"What for?"

"Lumber." He settled at the table and started eating.

Goddamn him, I thought, *and his bratty mood.*

"Jason." I took the chair across from him, damp dishtowel still in hand, voice short. "My brother's here, you know."

"I know."

"Well, do you think you can try to get along with me? At least this weekend?"

Silence.

"*Please*, Jason."

He stared ahead, took another bite of his sandwich, and chewed slowly and rhythmically. A crumb dangled from his mustache, and I wanted to slap it right off his smug face.

"Goddammit," I spewed through clenched teeth, startled by my sudden eruption. "Stop punishing me. Your timing sucks." I covered my face with my hands and squeezed my arms into my sides.

Before long, Jason came to my side of the table and rubbed my back. And then he sat down and draped his arm loosely around my shoulder while I stewed. I waited for him to say something, say anything. I wanted him to tell me how broken up he was about Carly, and I wanted—no, needed—to be told that I'd be okay.

And I'd want to believe it.

But the best Jason could do on that May afternoon was simply sit next to me.

"I'll try my best while your family's here," Jason finally spoke up, his terse voice breaking the silence. "But I told you this morning, I'm pissed, and I still am."

"Okay, Jason." I exhaled slowly. My shoulders slouched under the weight of aching fatigue.

We remained side by side, neither talking nor looking at each other, stewing in our mutual disappointment and exasperation. We were inches from each other in our little house, yet wholly alone.

Chapter 26—REUNION

~~~

The next afternoon I'd started boiling a bunch of potatoes for potato salad and shredding cabbage and carrots for coleslaw. In several hours, my entire extended family would be at my house for a wedding eve barbecue. Jason and Tom had taken Stacy and the kids to lunch, so I had the house to myself. I'd grown to appreciate time alone at home where I could openly commune with Carly, tell her that I missed her, and explain what she was missing.

"Your cousins are here," I said quietly at the sink, "and we're having a big party tonight. And if you're worried about your father and me, don't. I'll figure out how to keep the weekend calm."

The phone rang.

"Kristen, it's me." My friend Claire's New England accent was on the other end of the phone. She was a Boston friend I hadn't seen since moving to North Carolina, though we spoke occasionally on the phone, and a bit more after Carly died. "You're not going to believe this, but I'm driving through North Carolina. Care for a brief visit?"

"Well," I said, "the timing's kinda crazy."

"I'll stay just long enough for a hug. I've been dying to see you," Claire said.

When Claire arrived, she pulled me in for a long embrace. "I'm so glad to see you," she said. "I think about you all the time." Her fine wavy hair framed her large blue eyes and peaches-and-cream complexion.

"I'm glad to see you too," I said. "Do you want some iced tea? How are your girls?"

"They're fine. A handful. We're blessed," she said, climbing onto a stool at the kitchen bar. After requisite small talk about her small children, her husband's new job, and her dream to return to full-time nursing, Claire asked about me.

"Losing a baby must be so hard on couples."

"Yeah, it's been bumpy." I wasn't about to elaborate on the growing rancor between Jason and me when I needed to be cutting up potatoes, assembling coleslaw, and finishing a million other chores before guests arrived.

"I pray for you all the time," Claire said.

Unsolicited prayer seemed a close cousin to pity, and right or wrong, what my cynical brain heard was: *Your life is a mess, let me go ahead and ask a higher power to bail you out.* But I thanked Claire anyway, because what was I supposed to say? *How dare you pray for me? I'm fine!*

"I've prayed for you and Jason and Carly," Claire continued, "and I figured, why not tell you that in person on my drive back home."

Okay, I thought. *Duly noted.*

"Do you ever pray? Ever ask for help?"

The truth was I did not pray, and I asked no one for help. Nowhere in my history had prayer been introduced as a way to seek comfort. And asking for help? I was designed to put my head down and power through hardships.

"I don't pray, Claire, but I appreciate you doing so on my behalf."

"Since I'm here, how about I pray with you. Would you mind?"

Claire must have seen my hesitation, so she guided me to the sofa where we sat. She placed one hand over mine, another on my shoulder, and squeezed her eyelids shut. Lowering her head, she began speaking slowly.

"Lord, please look after my dear friend Kristen. She's had a hard time."

Claire continued her pleas for guidance and care for Carly, Jason, and me.

"Keep your light on them, Lord. Keep them near to you. When they feel weak, lift them up, breathe life into them. Help Kristen know that Carly is with you and is at peace."

Claire went on and on, earnest and determined and bold. Claustrophobia arrived, shrinking the sofa to a shoebox. My palms became clammy while the muggy air and stream of appeals made me feel conspicuous, exposed. What to do with myself during Claire's solo supplication? I fixed my eyes on the tops of my bare feet, on her hand over mine, and back to my feet. I waited.

Claire finally stopped, opened her eyes, and smiled. "Hope that wasn't too strange."

Desperate for space, I got up. "Let's go."

I led Claire on a ten-minute tour of our small house, and when we climbed up to the loft, Claire noticed Carly's picture sitting on my desk.

"Is that her? Can I take a look?"

Just that morning, Jason and I had avoided a fight about the photo.

"What's this doing here?" he'd asked, pointing to the pink frame on the top shelf in his office.

"I don't want to leave her picture in our bedroom while Tom and Stacy are here."

"Well, you should have told me," Jason snapped, turning away.

"I did."

"Well, I forgot. Jesus."

Jason was Carly's father, so why did I have to shield her photo from him? As far as baby pictures went, I understood from the start that for some, hers was charged. Evidently, even for Jason. To this day, I keep the small frame out of the public view; I can't bear to sense anyone's unease when looking at my child.

Claire held Carly's photo, her eyes moving back and forth across the image. "You know, she looks serene. I believe Carly's in a better place right now and that someday you'll understand why she died."

"I hope so," I said, taking the frame and returning it to the shelf. I didn't want Carly's face scrutinized and read like tea leaves. I wanted her left alone.

The farewell hug I gave Claire in the driveway was quick, and as much I loved her, I was glad she was leaving. I had known her long enough to understand that her intentions behind visiting were good, but her visit felt confusing and intrusive. I wanted to be thankful for Claire's prayers, and hell, maybe I would have participated if I'd been given a choice. But the unbidden invocation felt like a well-meaning yet clumsily executed intervention. Before returning to the kitchen, and to the potatoes and cabbage, and to all the other barbecue duties that awaited me, I returned to the loft and hugged Carly's photo against my chest.

"I'm sorry," I whispered. "For everything."

⁓

When my house filled up with family a few hours later, Jason found his smile and gave it away freely: at the grill where he bragged good-naturedly about his famous marinade, playing croquet, talking with my father. He even smiled at me a few times as he handed me platters of cooked meat. I didn't care if his improved mood was authentic or manufactured, I was glad he showed up to the party and relieved we could hide our tension from my family.

In the months after Carly's death, I'd been with almost all of my family in separate visits, but now we were completely together under one roof. The few who hadn't yet seen me seemed initially nervous, as just about everybody in the world had those early days. I'd often wonder about this fear. Did people worry that I might erupt into wails? That they'd fumble with their words? That there are wrong words, right words, any words to capture the injustice of a baby's death? I knew there was nothing to say. So I learned the steps to the awkward dance of first encounters. Smile, let my uneasy partner speak or not if she wanted, thank her for whatever words she could find, and then carefully move together toward our new normal. At the party, I understood that for guests to enjoy themselves and for me to feel connected to them, I'd need to set the tone. As the evening unfolded, I laughed many times from moments of genuine delight, like playing rousing games of badminton and joking with my brothers. Claire's odd visit seemed distant, and the glimpse of a relaxed Jason helped me to push our troubles aside at least for now. The pain of Carly's absence didn't disappear, but I also felt happy. Watching my niece chase my nephew around the yard was so painfully cute, I wanted to burst. The bereft, I'd come to understand, don't feel *only* sad; we sometimes feel *more* of *everything*.

Cole let me hold him after dinner. Enough time had passed in his one-year-old eyes to leave his parents' arms. While family milled about eating brownies and ice cream, he sat on my lap. I bounced him up and down, his little feet pushing against my thighs so he could stand. He giggled as I kissed his warm, soft neck and breathed in his sweet baby smells. Jason, never able to resist a laughing baby, joined us, sending Cole into happy squeals with every tickle of his belly. I'm sure my family took notice of the scene: the baby-less parents playing with a baby. Did they think I was dying inside, wishing I were holding my own child?

I wasn't.

I could not imbue any feelings of Carly onto Cole. He was too big, older than Carly would have been and already his own person. But when David and Kate's child was born a year and a half later, I did struggle. Holding my niece as an infant petrified me. I remember sitting stiffly with her in my arms in her first weeks, relieved when someone came by and scooped her up. I wanted to touch the feathery down on her head and the smooth skin of her cheeks, letting the weight of her small body meld into mine. But all I could do was listen to my own amped-up heartbeat and will it to slow down. *Please be alive,* I once silently pleaded as she lay motion-less in my arms. *Make a sound, move your finger, flutter an eyelid.* Not until Lila smiled and cooed and seemed less like the tiniest of newborns could my muscles relax and my mind stop spinning.

The evening waned, and one by one my family left, hugging Jason and me and thanking us for hosting.

"No problem," I said. "It was fun. See you tomorrow."

"Sleep well," Tom said as he carried Cole down the hall to join Stacy and Tatum. "Tonight was great." And he disappeared into my bedroom.

Alone, Jason and I stood awkwardly in the living room.

"Well, we pulled it off," I said.

"Yup," Jason agreed and placed his hand on my shoulder. "Good party."

We looked at each other cautiously, neither one of us willing or brave enough to smile.

"I'll be up in a minute," Jason finally said.

I undressed and lay on top of the air mattress, the air steamy and thick. How would I ever sleep in this heat? I listened as Jason's computer booted up, as his desk chair creaked when he rocked back and forth, and as he clicked away on his keyboard typing who knows what to whom.

"Hey Claire," I whispered, "would you mind sending a prayer for Jason to sleep in the office tonight?"

Chapter 27—GOATS

~~~~~

The sun poured through the small loft window early in the morning, and I looked at Jason sleeping next to me. His mouth was slightly ajar and the ends of his mustache hooked over his lip. I realized he was the only man I knew who still wore a mustache. And I loathed it.

I tiptoed to my desk and opened my journal.

Good Morning, Carly. Today is the big day. I wish you could be with us, with me, wrapped in my arms, perched on my hip, loved on by my family. You deserved to know what a big celebration is like, but I will enjoy myself enough for the both of us.

Down in the kitchen I started a pot of coffee when Tom poked his head around the corner.

"They're all still sleeping. Thank God." He smiled. "I mean, I love them, but a little space sometimes is a really good thing."

"I hear you," I said. "Hey, drive with me to the wedding."

The outdoor ceremony was forty miles south of Chapel Hill at a rural bed and breakfast.

"What about Jason? And Stacy and the kids?"

"I think you and I should get there early," I lied, "to help set up. Jason can drive everyone closer to the start of the ceremony."

Tom didn't need to know that I was looking for ways to avoid Jason, that sleeping together on that teeny air mattress was closer to him than I wanted to be, that an hour in the car together would feel like an eternity.

———

We parked in an expansive field and walked through the freshly mown grass to the main house of the bed and breakfast, a traditional farmhouse with a large wraparound porch, spider plants hanging from the posts, and pink and white geraniums lining the steps. The temperature was balmy. Tom went inside while I grabbed a glass of lemonade from the bar and followed the bleating cries of goats. A dozen gray-and-brown babies tromped around a small, grass-filled pen, and they were noisy and busy, soft ears flopping as they hurried from one side of the pen to another. A few looked up and even pushed their noses toward me and sniffed my fingers. Beside the pen was a short row of logs. I sat on one and faced the goats as if watching a play.

The lemonade cooled my throat as I stared down at my unpainted toenails poking through my sandals. I had been a regular at my old nail salon in Boston, keeping my toes pedicured all summer long. I would have felt sloppy otherwise. But I hadn't stepped into a salon or felt pretty or dressed up in forever. My formerly always-highlighted hair had gotten no more attention in the last year than twenty-dollar cuts from walk-in salons. My natural rodent-brown shade looked duller than ever.

I tried to rally before the wedding by buying a new outfit and sandals, and even pulled out eyeliner and eye shadow. But the extra makeup and new pink blouse didn't help me feel any less frumpy. I still carried extra weight, still wore the same old stretched-out bra from when I was pregnant. I sagged. I had a speaking part in the ceremony, would have to trek all the way to the altar, turn around, and face the guests: Here I am everyone, a Plain Jane who botched up her life! "Oh, that's David sister," somebody would murmur. "She's the one whose baby was still-born. Poor thing."

Losing a baby is only the half of it, I imagined telling a sympathetic wedding guest. *You should have seen Jason's explosion with our therapist the other night.*

I swallowed the last of my lemonade and stuck a few fingers through the pen and watched the smallest goat in the bunch, cream colored with the quietest voice. "Come here, little guy," I said. "Let me pet your tiny nose." He didn't budge, but a chocolate brown fellow trotted to my hand. I rubbed the top of his ear for a few seconds before he darted away.

———

About eighty of us, all dressed in requisite spring pastels and flo-rals, sat on white folding chairs facing the spacious wraparound porch. An aisle cut down the middle of the chairs and led to the altar, a small linen-covered table with flowers and candles. Chickens clucked, and an occasional hen wandered away from her nearby henhouse and circulated among the guests' legs. Tom and I sat next to each other in the front row while the rest of my family sat behind us. Jason was toward the middle.

The service featured a few guitar-strumming musicians, a Unitarian minister, and a time for guests to share sentiments about David and Kate. This was the segment I introduced, and I recall nothing of it. Years later I barely recognized myself in the photo taken of me at the altar, microphone in hand and corsage pinned crooked on my pink floral top. Though my cheeks are rosy and lips are covered in shimmery gloss, my eyes betray an obvious exhaustion. The shadows underneath are a giveaway, but my blank expression is what makes me look flat and lifeless.

Tom spoke next. He stood up and extended Dave and Kate's love to family and friends who couldn't attend—an elderly grandmother, a traveling college roommate. "And we wish Carly were with us today as well," Tom said at the very end, his voice shaking. David had asked if I'd wanted Carly's name included in the service: I did and welcomed hearing it spoken.

The ceremony closed with music, clapping, cheering, and hugs. As I mingled with my family, Jason walked toward me.

"Kris." He threw his arms around me and whispered into my ear, "I love you. I'm sorry." His body trembled while silvery tears streamed down his face. *Oh no*, I thought. *Why's he crying?* My family quietly backed away. I closed my eyes and let Jason hug me. But my arms remained limp at my side, and I said not a word. I only waited for him to release his grip on my back.

Jason's eyes were red and puffy and his nose dripped. I pulled a tissue out of my purse and handed it to him. "Did you know Tom was going to mention Carly?" Jason asked, wiping his face, "because I didn't. As soon as I heard her name. Whoa."

And with that, another round of tears.

By now, all the wedding guests had migrated to the patio on the opposite side of the house, and I wished I were with them instead of supplying Jason with tissues.

"I love you, Kris," he said again, rubbing his hands on my back. "And I love Carly too. We're going to get through this, I promise you. Do you hear me?"

All his rage from two days ago—where was it today?

"Sure." I shrugged, looking not at his eyes, but at the cuffs of his khaki suit pants resting atop his shiny dress shoes. I wanted to put an end to our embarrassing scene.

"We'll be fine," Jason said again. "Okay? Do you believe me?"

"Hey, Kris," my brother Tom yelled from the porch. "Time for pictures. Come on up."

My memories of the reception are fragmented. Musicians played guitars, flute, and harmonica on the patio as twilight bathed the sky in hazy blues. My niece squealed at a chicken that ambled too close to her skinny legs. A small throng of children mixed in with adults on the dance floor, flailing their arms, twisting their torsos, and lifting up their skirts and shirts to stay cool. My brother danced with me, as did my father, and I laughed and smiled and savored the freedom of being out of my head and in my body, of feeling the bond to my family.

I talked to a guest who had sent me a letter after Carly died. Years earlier her baby girl had died, and I'd been grateful for her kind and hopeful sympathy card. Her clear blue eyes and porcelain skin struck me, and I thanked her for reaching out, hoping I might actually have a new friend in the making.

I shared my slide show. Guests gathered under the gazebo while my laptop projected the photos onto a large screen. The music I'd added to the presentation created a happy depiction of the bride's and groom's lives. I pictured the angel that had appeared when I'd created the slide show at Kinko's weeks earlier. Pressing my hands together, I took in a long breath and sent Carly a message: *I'm here, baby girl, wishing you were with me.*

Toward the end of the reception, I sat alone at the edge of the dance floor and recalled how I used to manage large parties. I was never an attention-getter in a crowd, but I navigated social scenes with ease, innately knowing how to start conversations and joke among people I didn't know terribly well. Now small talk was a strain. Jason was bopping and swaying about with fellow dancers. His jacket was off, shirtsleeves rolled up past his elbows, and hair streaked with sweat. His limbs hung loose, like he'd had plenty of beer.

"Jason sure knows how to have fun," my mother said. "Just look at him out there."

The wedding was not the time to spill the truth about Jason's ever-changing moods of indifference, rage, despair, and now glee. My mother and I would talk soon enough.

Back at home in Chapel Hill, Stacy and Tom slouched at the kitchen table with bloodshot eyes and glasses of water.

"I'll see you in the morning," Stacy said. "I've got to get some sleep." She and Tom walked down the hall toward my bedroom, Stacy's high heels dangling in one hand, her other gripping my brother's elbow.

Except for his crying stretch at the wedding, Jason and I were alone for the first time.

"Did you have fun?" Jason asked, leaning against the counter, his shirt untucked and tie askew around his neck. His eyes drooped from fatigue but looked soft, as if the deluge of tears had unearthed his long-absent sweet side.

"I think everyone had fun," I answered. "Did you?"

"Yeah. I did. The dancing felt great. I needed to relax and let go."

"Good. I'm glad."

Jason grabbed my arm. "Kris?"

"What?"

"Can we hug?"

I stepped forward and let him pull me in, let him nuzzle his nose into my hair and neck. I felt the muscles of my back let go as I leaned on his chest, the iron in my neck and shoulders softening. Truce. When we climbed onto the air mattress, I didn't roll away from him. I let him rest his leg against mine while I held his hand and listened to his breathing get deeper and slower. Sleep took him under first, and we lay together like an ordinary couple, exhausted after a big wedding.

—⚬—

The sound of the shower running downstairs woke me in the morning. Tatum chattered to my brother who said little besides, "Yes sweetie" or "Hand me that bag," and an occasional, "Quiet down." Even though I was in the loft, I could sense Tom's pre-flight tension and knew he was anxious to hurry Stacy out of the shower, pack up the car, and take off. Jason continued to slumber while my brother's voice downstairs grew louder. "Hurry up, Stace. We've got to get going."

Time to say good-bye. I swung my legs over the side of the mattress and reached for my robe. My hair felt dirty after a full day of North Carolina heat and humidity, and I pulled it back with an elastic band. Out in the driveway, the sendoff was frenetic and quick. I held Cole while Tom and Stacy loaded the minivan, and Tatum dawdled behind them, her pink backpack strapped tightly on her shoulders. Jason emerged from the back door and stood beside me, his hair as rumpled as his T-shirt and shorts. There were hugs and kisses and promises to call later. A stinging pressure built behind my eyes, and I pressed my lips together as Tom buckled his seat belt and started the engine, as Stacy passed a sippy cup back to Cole, and as the van disappeared out of sight.

I went directly to the shower. Once I saw steam rise from behind the curtain, I dropped my robe and stepped inside. Warm water splashed against my skin as I rested my forehead against the tile wall. Crying started up and steady sobs soon echoed around me. The wedding was over, my family was gone, and Jason and I would be alone again with nothing but our heartache and bust-ed-up relationship. The day loomed ahead, weeks loomed ahead, and in that moment, my entire future seemed endlessly empty.

Jason had gone off somewhere, and I lumbered through the afternoon alone. I washed the sheets and lay down for a nap, my limbs too cumbersome and heavy to carry around all day. I cleaned the kitchen, sorted through the mail, and tried to ignore the strain in my chest by watching the Food Network on TV. But the young, beautiful Italian chef effortlessly chopping onions with a bright smile on her face, her kitchen gleaming in the background, left me feeling jealous and inept. Out the window, finches alit on the dogwood, their little throats pumping up and down pushing their songs out through their beaks. What were they so happy about?

Like sporadic rain from a stubborn storm, tears came and went throughout the day. Periods of calm were interrupted by periods of misery. Tears fell for my missing child, the one in the flesh I'd held so briefly, and for her spirit, wherever and what-ever it was. Even if Carly were in a blissful state of divinity, as I wanted to believe, she would be far from me forever. I was trapped living in a mundane, tedious world without her, search-ing for ways to keep us together. Tears of self-pity fell, the hardest kind to stop. I missed myself, the version of me before Carly died—maybe even the version of me before I left Boston—and I wept because I knew there was no returning. A bone-weary fatigue took hold of me, and I wept because I felt much older than my thirty-nine years.

It was a bad day made worse by my own judgment about it. Wasn't I supposed to be getting better? Hadn't I just pulled off the slew of wedding events? What about the therapy I'd been doing and the reams of journal entries? They were supposed to keep me moving forward. Much later, I understood that rogue surges of grief would show up unexpectedly. Therapy, journaling, and even Time, the Universal Healer would not protect me from a lurch back to profound mourning. Sometimes I'd be cruising along perfectly happy and yet somehow stumble into a dolorous ditch. Listless and sluggish and in the dark, I'd find my way back to the light. And I'd learn to do this again and again.

Chapter 28—TEST

Was I really about to buy this?

I stared at a pregnancy test kit in my hand. I'd finally looked at a calendar after the wedding and realized that, despite my no longer predictable period, I was officially late. Too late to ignore.

The local CVS was old and dingy, and I never wanted to loiter. But I could not yet bear to stand in the register line with my pregnancy test, so I procrastinated in the aisle, enduring the saccharine pop music reverberating around me. We used condoms, didn't we? Maybe we were lazy once or twice? When had we even last been together?

Early after Carly's death, others expected that Jason and I would not only try for parenthood again, but would succeed. I allowed friends to offer up the idea of motherhood with a living baby. A new baby—certainly not a replacement—was carefully and repeatedly laid before me like a promissory note I could cash in for the life I was due. Hell, at my six-week postpartum checkup, my midwife had volunteered, "For your next pregnancy, we'll keep a closer eye on you, probably order more ultrasounds, and induce you early."

Is she kidding me? I'd thought, shocked at her assumption that I'd sign up for pregnancy again, shocked at her optimism.

When I'd handed the buxom young receptionist my copay, she'd asked how my baby was doing, no doubt a standard question when "postpartum visit" was circled on the invoice.

She shuffled papers and lowered her eyes when I told her that Carly had died. I'd wanted to apologize.

A small elderly woman behind me touched my elbow.

"Well, your next one will be just fine," she said, "and the one after that, too."

"That's right," the receptionist declared, looking up again with a reassuring smile. "You'll have more."

It seemed baby number two was a given for just about everyone. But how could I stay connected with Carly if I were pregnant again? When Jason and I had re-bonded in the early months after Carly's death, the notion of a future pregnancy sailed in front of us like a leaf caught in a breeze: fleeting and delicate and hard to grasp. Maybe we should try again? Skip a condom? Maybe not? Get a condom? But once our relationship was wobbling, we both knew that one baby was plenty for us, even if she'd died. Besides, what I clutched at was the promise of a lighter future, where I woke up with purpose and a smile. Maybe Jason felt the same.

I walked the pregnancy test and myself to the front of the store and handed the young CVS salesgirl my credit card.

"Will this be it?" Her fingers punched confidently at the register.

Good question, I thought.

"Jason, I have something to tell you."

We were on the deck, about to eat a pizza dinner, a trio of fireflies buzzing in and out of the nearby tree branches. My belly gurgled, too nervous to take a bite.

"Yeah? What?"

Jason's cathartic crying at the wedding had left him in an elevated mood, and he smiled, running his bare foot along my shin. I was glad for the shift, though I didn't trust it would last. Especially now.

"I took a pregnancy test today."

His foot slowly dropped from my leg and he sat up straight. I looked first at him and then into the branches following the path of the fireflies.

"You're kidding."

"Nope."

Silence. We sat together sullen, pizza untouched. In the hours between the pregnancy test and dinner, I'd kept the news to myself, too stunned to feel a thing. Now that Jason knew, the truth started chipping away at my numbed state and the floodgates of worry opened. How could I possibly handle this? Nine months all over again? This couldn't be happening.

"Well," Jason finally said, "we'll make this work. Somehow." But his flat voice gave him away and scared me. He was feeling the same dread. *I'm too tired, I'm too tired, I'm too tired* ran through my head as I pictured myself managing everything again, stitching together another plan for another baby while Jason stumbled along trying to earn an income.

"When's it due?" Jason reached for a slice of pizza.

"Somewhere in February, I think."

Just after what would have been Carly's first birthday, I thought with a pang of guilt.

"Jesus, I wasn't expecting this." Jason sighed. "Why didn't you tell me you were late?"

"I didn't realize how late I was. My period isn't predictable anymore, and I guess I was preoccupied by the wedding."

Plus, I wanted to say, *even if I had checked my calendar a week or two ago, when would I have told you? Between which fights?*

Jason closed his eyes, dropped back in his chair, and let out a loud sigh. Given that I could practically see his newfound sunnier disposition leak out like a deflating balloon, why didn't I shut up? Why didn't I let the news of another pregnancy be enough for one night? But I blurted, "I'm going to need a lot more support from you this time."

Jason turned to me slowly, and then without saying a word, got up, pushed in his chair, and walked into the house, slamming the door behind him.

My heartbeat picked up.

Minutes later, Jason returned, duffel bag in hand, face as red as blood.

"I tried my best, Kris," he fumed. "Too bad you never noticed."

"I'm sorry," I stammered. "It didn't come out right. What I meant to say is that I'm upset."

"Bullshit. Bullshit. *Bull. Shit.* You're never satisfied."

"Not true."

"I'm leaving," he said, "and you know what else? I don't think we should be together. At all."

He drove off.

I found my way to bed, covered myself in a blanket, and lay still while thoughts ricocheted: *I'm pregnant. How will I do this? I don't want to do this. I'm sorry, Carly. Where is Jason? Will he come back?* A mere one week earlier I had not wanted to be near Jason at all. Now I wanted him home.

I catnapped until dawn when I got up for good, my muscles stiff and thoughts muddled. I brushed my teeth without looking at my reflection, not wanting to see my haggard face. The pregnancy stick was in the bathroom trash can where yesterday I'd stared in shock at the results. Looking at it one more time confirmed that yes, I was still fertile. And also a fool.

Crimson- and coral-streaked clouds lit up a patch of sky beyond my driveway where my car spent the night alone. This irritated me, this dawn of a beautiful morning. I wanted to cry out: "Stop carrying on as if everything's fine."

My mind leapt between anxieties: how on earth would I manage a pregnancy, how would I ever get my life calmed down, and how would I deal with Jason? While channel surfing between identical-looking morning news shows outlining the chaos of the Iraqi war, I told myself that Jason would have to come home sooner or later. When he did finally return, he walked through the back door and went directly to his office. No greeting.

"Jason." I stood in the doorway, his back to me as he waited for his computer to boot up. "Where did you go last night?"

No response.

"Jason."

Silence.

He put one hand on his mouse and wiggled it back and forth while his computer came to life. With his other hand he adjusted his baseball cap.

"You won't talk?" My voice cracked. "Come on. Please."

Jason's fingers clacked at the keyboard. I glanced at the computer screen and watched as letters and words filled an email window. I wanted to scream, snatch the keyboard, and throw it to the floor, spinning him around in his chair until he looked at me. But I did nothing. Jason wasn't going to budge, I knew this.

"Goddamn you," was all I said and went to the kitchen, the room designated as mine when we engaged in silent prizefights.

After forcing down a bowl of cereal and loading the dishwasher, I heard Jason's footsteps walking down the hall.

"We'll make this work," Jason said for the second time in twelve hours as we stared at each other from across the kitchen table. And even though I doubted him, his overture toward collaboration was a comfort.

"Yeah. We will," I practically whispered. "We'll have to."

"I'm going to work in my office today," Jason said.

"Sure," I said. "I've got a few things to do today anyway."

But I lied. I had nothing to do, other than walk on tenterhooks with Jason and try not to feel sorry for myself, for Carly, and for the newest life forming inside me.

CHAPTER 29—ESCAPE

Two days later, I called my boss to tell her I could not attend a professional training she'd arranged for me in Atlanta. The program began that weekend, and the idea of navigating not only a six-hour drive solo, but also a three-day training without knowing a soul felt dizzying. Small talk? Trying to focus? And alone?

"Don't worry," she said. "These courses are offered all the time. Take care of yourself, and we'll sign you up again when you're ready."

She was compassionate, thank goodness, and had eased my return to work after Carly died by bringing me lunches and allowing me to leave early or arrive late if my mood was particularly raw. If she was fazed by news of my latest pregnancy and my abrupt change of plans, she didn't flinch.

"You're squandering the opportunity to advance your career?" Jason said that evening when I told him my change of plans. He stared at me, slack-jawed with brows creased. "I can't believe this. You talked all spring about these classes."

"I'll take them later," I said.

"But won't this training boost your salary? We need the money."

I didn't respond. Every topic was evidently fair game for a fight, and one small misstep would cause the house of cards we lived in to buckle and fall around us.

"So that's it?" he snapped, his stare penetrating. "You're quitting?"

Not quitting, I thought, *but not talking to you anymore.* Turning on my heels, I marched down the hall, grabbed my purse, and walked out the back door, the moonlit gravel driveway crunching under my flip-flops. I gently tapped on my brother's front door, my guilt at barging in within hours of his return from his honeymoon pierced deeper when I saw luggage piled in the entryway. He had barely been home, probably hadn't opened the wedding gifts yet, and in walked the needy sister.

"I'm sorry," I blubbered as I crumbled in his office. "My timing sucks."

"It's okay," he said. "What happened?"

"I have to get away from Jason," I spewed, "and I'm pregnant again."

I confessed the truth about the last months to David: the fights and the mood swings. Unloading was a slow relief, and David's wide eyes validated that I was living in a tsunami.

"I don't know what to do."

"About another baby?"

"About everything."

"Do you want this baby?"

"I wanted Carly," my voice cracked. "But I won't abort, if that's what you're wondering. I've had enough death for one year."

I didn't want to be pregnant, certainly not with Jason and maybe not ever, but I wasn't about to deny a chance to the clump of cells in my womb, not after Carly's chance of life was denied after her forty-one weeks of hard work for nothing.

"Well, you won't figure everything out tonight," David said. "Why don't you sleep here?"

"Thanks." I forced a smile. "Was the trip good?" Already the wedding seemed far away.

While he rooted through his linen closet for an extra blanket and pillow, I looked out the window toward my house. Jason's truck was still in the driveway and his office light was on. Did he even know I was gone?

I must have switched positions in bed and adjusted my pillow dozens of times; sleep was not going to arrive anytime soon. The streetlight shining through the slats of the blinds cast yellow-tinted stripes on the wall. I tried counting them. Finally, I flipped open my cell phone to check the time: Nine forty-five. Not too late to make a call.

"Mom," I said softly.

I told her everything.

"Come to New York," she said. "I'll buy the ticket."

"Thank you," I whispered and hung up, realizing I hadn't caught her reaction to my being pregnant.

The night dragged out as I mulled over what I would say to Jason in the morning. He would seem indifferent when I told him I was going to New York, but I guessed that he would truly be angry. For a fleeting moment I worried about leaving my cats in his care. Would he remember to feed them, scoop the litter, and keep them inside? And then my thoughts landed back in familiar territory. What must Carly think? I felt her watching my interior life, like I imagined she had when I was pregnant. Perhaps if she had lived even for a little while on her own, I might have seen her as separate. But I only ever knew her as a being within me, and she remained that way, even after her small body was long gone.

"This is not a replacement baby," I closed my eyes and whispered into the night. "Okay? You'll always be my girl."

And then I pushed a finger into the side of a breast. Not nearly as sore as when I was pregnant with Carly. Same with the other one. Maybe this pregnancy would feel different. I placed my hand on my belly and whispered again, "I'll make room for you, too."

But how?

Chapter 30—MOTHER

~~~~~~~

My eyes scanned the crowd at the baggage terminal until they fixed on my mother. Her purse hung from her shoulder while she waved, and I felt myself relax like a child reuniting with a parent at the bus stop after a long, hard day at school.

"I scheduled a massage for you," she said as we drove toward her new downsized house. Thank goodness, because my neck and shoulders had been seized since I awoke in David's office. I could barely turn my head.

Jason's reaction to my spontaneous New York trip had gone as I'd predicted. "Fine," he'd said coolly, staring into his coffee cup, placing his cap on his head and turning away. "I don't understand, but fine."

I'd quickly packed a bag and then gone to an appointment with my therapist Victor before heading to the airport. I'd sat on the edge of his leather couch and stared at his Ansel Adams calendar displaying Yosemite's Half Dome bathed in grays and white.

"I feel like I'm living on the brink," I sobbed, stuffing my purse with one damp tissue after another.

"And you can't live on the brink forever, can you?" he'd asked.

Exactly the problem, I thought as I flew out of North Carolina, the very place I had escaped to the last time I was on the edge. How to get back on steady ground?

My mother's modest suburban neighborhood consisted of soaring elm trees lining the streets, and a mix of split-level ranch and Cape-style homes. Once settled, I left her house twice: to buy prenatal vitamins at CVS, and to get the massage. Because my mother worked full time, I spent the days padding around her house alone, reading, watching television, writing in my journal. In one of my segments to Carly, I let her know I'd escaped to New York:

> You've got a sibling on the way. I'm at your grand-
> mother's house, trying to figure out how to make room
> for him. Without crowding you out. Complicated.

I struggled to imagine the bliss of cradling a living baby in nine months. If there was a portion of my heart reserved for children, Carly occupied the entirety of it. I couldn't visualize how any other baby, even the one growing inside me, could possibly change that. Besides, being pregnant seemed only like another problem to solve, like the hostility between Jason and me.

"What'd you do today?" my mother asked in the evenings. She'd return from work to find me in sweatpants and T-shirts, my hair pulled away from my wan face with bobby pins or a ponytail. Compared to my mother, who wore makeup and office attire and who came home fresh from interactions with the outside world, I was a lifeless lump planted on her furniture each day.

"I finished a book."

I'd found Anita Shreve's *Fortune's Rocks* on my mother's bookshelf, the story of a young, unmarried, nineteenth-century New England girl whose life crashed around her after becoming pregnant. *Ironic*, I thought. I couldn't put the book down.

"And I watched Ronald Reagan's funeral."

My mother's eyes revealed disbelief.

"There was nothing else on. Daytime television sucks."

Ronald Reagan was the president of my college years. My liberal New England classmates and I had disliked his conservative policies and had made fun of his sing-songy voice and Nancy's "Just Say No" campaign. Yet twenty years later, sprawled on my mother's floral sofa, I watched the proceedings from start to finish, shedding tears when Nancy laid her small head atop her husband's casket, the dramatic finale.

My mother and I talked little about Jason and me and my pregnancy. She knew I'd need time with my own thoughts before I could share them. Other than inquiring about my physical symptoms, she didn't probe.

And at my mother's house, I had plenty of space and solitude. I was no longer gripped with anxiety as I had been a few days earlier, and a resignation settled in that Jason and I would never return to a peaceable state.

On a warm, clear June afternoon, I sat at a picnic table in my mother's backyard, brilliant color everywhere. The emerald-green lawn was edged with purple irises, orange day lilies, yellow daisies, and a white picket fence. Under the azure sky, I considered options to possibly manage this baby on my own. Maybe I'd find a less expensive rental in Chapel Hill, quit my UNC job, and return to full-time teaching. Somehow I'd afford childcare, food, utilities, baby supplies, and an occasional new blouse. My brother might offer periodic babysitting on a Saturday afternoon so I could run errands. I'd find a community of single mothers, and we'd create child-care co-ops.

I imagined teaching again in my former school district in Massachusetts. Picking up where I'd left off in my former life, I'd earn a decent salary once again and provide for my child. But wouldn't moving our baby hours away from North Carolina be unfair to Jason? And could I tolerate those interminable bleak winters?

Closing my eyes, I pictured the landscape of my childhood: the small beaches dotting the shoreline, the whistle of the train as it trundled into town, the delis, pizza, and bagels. I hadn't lived on Long Island since graduating from high school twenty-two years earlier, nor had I wanted to. But on that June day in 2004 in my mother's backyard, I thought, *What's wrong with this*? My mother's house, though humble, had two large guest bedrooms and a bathroom upstairs—more than enough space for a baby and me. Could I convince my mother to turn her quiet, on-the-verge-of-retirement life upside down, and welcome her grandchild and me into her home? In exchange, I'd shop, cook, and clean. Nothing new there. To earn side money, I'd tutor schoolchildren until I could return to full-time teaching and find my own home. *This might work*, I thought. A picture of a manageable and happier future began taking shape, and I already felt relief from my imagined plan.

The phone rang through the open kitchen window, interrupting my fantasy.

"Kris," my mother said, "Jason just called me."

"What? How did he get your office number?" I asked, stretching the yellow cord of her telephone so I could sit at her kitchen table.

"Don't know. He wants you to call him. He sounded weird."

"Great," I muttered.

We hadn't talked since I'd left Chapel Hill, and I'd told him not to expect to hear from me. I stood up and paced, looping several times through the dining room, living room, and back to the kitchen. Would he still be angry with me for canceling the training? In the midst of a crying spell, filled with remorse and sadness? Frustrated because his truck broke down yet again? Was one of my cats sick?

"What do you mean where was I?" I asked when I finally called Jason back.

"I tried your cell phone this morning and again at lunch. No answer."

"I didn't hear it. It's upstairs in my purse. I was probably in the shower."

"Well, where were you today?"

"Here."

"Doing what?"

"Nothing. Why are you grilling me?" I let out an impatient sigh and tapped my finger on the kitchen table.

"I just find it hard to believe you can't hear your phone. Your mother's house isn't that big." He sounded testy. "Are you avoiding me? Did you go out somewhere?"

Maybe Jason wanted to push me further away. Perhaps he wanted to be done with our trouble-laden life, and now that his second baby was growing inside me, he'd grabbed the most direct exit he could find.

"Have you seen any old boyfriends while in New York?"

"That's right," I practically hooted. "Everything's been so dull since Carly died, I thought I'd stir things up and try reconnecting with an old flame. And hell, my current circumstances make me a real catch."

Jason did not reply.

"I'll tell you what I have been doing. Figuring out how to rebuild my life. That's it."

We hung up, and I stewed on my mother's front stoop. I watched neighborhood children walk home from school, swinging their backpacks, spontaneously erupting into laughter or skipping. *My God, they have so much energy*, I thought. *Did I really used to teach all day long*? One by one these children peeled off and raced down a driveway. One last girl ambled up the street, ebony braids flopping against her shoulders as she kicked a stone from one side of the road to the other. She glanced up intermittently, aiming for a spot along the curb before she drew her skinny leg back and then flung it forward, her purple sneaker sending the stone barreling ahead. Back and forth this girl went, unwavering in her zig-zaggy route home.

"I can't be in Chapel Hill all summer," I said aloud. I returned inside, logged onto my mother's computer in her puny office, and emailed six different friends in Boston. By the end of the day I had finalized plans for another trip.

Chapter 31—ALIEN

"More ginger ale, ma'am?" the flight attendant asked on her way up the aisle.

"No thank you, I'm set," I said and handed her my empty cup with a pretzel wrapper balled up inside. I returned to watching the vast clouds through the small airplane window, and imagined my happy reunion with friends and the city I missed.

In the short time I was home in Chapel Hill between New York and Boston, Jason and I had settled into a ceasefire. We barely spoke of the pregnancy or discussed my escape to New York. Jason worked small carpentry jobs here and there during the day, television was our chaperone until bedtime, and after a polite goodnight, we stuck to our sides of the bed.

"I probably won't call much when I'm gone," I'd said to Jason when he dropped me off at the airport.

"Not expecting you to."

"Okay, well, see you in ten days."

I'd chosen ginger ale among the drink selections offered by the flight attendant in case I became suddenly nauseated. But the positive pregnancy test was so far the only evidence I was experiencing. My midwife practice had transferred me to an ob-gyn at the hospital because my pregnancy was officially considered high risk. I saw Dr. Carter for my first prenatal visit before the Boston trip. A pretty young professional, her black polka-dot dress and pearls visible underneath her white lab coat offered a stark contrast to the earthy midwives in their clogs, ponytails, and mascara-free lashes.

"You're going to be seeing a lot of us," she said with a warm smile. "More ultrasounds, an amniocentesis, and we'll induce you at thirty-eight weeks."

"I figured." I pushed away the memory of the deafening silence of my last ultrasound, the one that had searched in vain for Carly's heartbeat. How would I survive a series of ultrasounds in the coming months?

"Stillbirths as late in the game as you experienced are uncommon, and according to your records, there hadn't been any cause for concern. But we're still going to be extra careful this time around."

"I understand."

And I did. With my history, no doctor would "proceed as normal" with my prenatal care. This fetus would be intruded upon for reasons I couldn't argue against. Still, not for one moment did I believe different prenatal care would have changed Carly's outcome. I didn't need the autopsy report to confirm what I knew in my bones: I was healthy and so was she, right up until her final heartbeat. Jason had sequestered himself in his office one evening, pored over the report, and read every single line in the pages and pages of medical jargon. Not me. While I wondered what had caused that little muscle in her chest to stop pumping, I knew Carly had merely decided she was done with this life. Why she had left and where she'd gone were my questions.

So I resigned myself to let Dr. Carter create a safety plan for this new baby, though I didn't feel any safer. Babies die.

Dr. Carter's eyes filled as our session ended. "I'm sorry," she said, bringing a knuckle to her outer eye to catch a tear. "I feel for you. This must be hard."

"Thanks." I smiled, appreciating her ability to speak to me as one woman to another. But I couldn't help but feel pressure that if my life didn't start looking normal, nice people like Dr. Carter would give up on me. I'd be The Lost Cause. The One Who'd Had So Much Promise.

Maybe this baby would vindicate me.

———— ❦ ————

Leslie and I sat on the deck of her third-floor apartment and looked out over her Cambridge neighborhood. The air was dry and comfortable, so unlike steamy North Carolina. Voices from pedestrians below floated up to our perch.

"I don't have the same symptoms as before," I told her as we munched on cheese and crackers, Leslie sipping wine while I stuck with water. Leslie was a teacher friend, single, and we'd connected over our amusing days with ten-year-olds. The news of another pregnancy didn't alarm her. She was always confident that I could handle whatever life threw my way.

"What do you mean?"

"I'm not nauseated, I'm not tired, and my boobs aren't sore."

"Isn't each pregnancy different?" Leslie asked. "Maybe it's a boy. Your dates could be off. Why don't you call your doctor when you get back and ask for an ultrasound."

"I'm already on deck for a bunch of ultrasounds," I said, tucking my feet underneath me on her brown wicker chair. "And my doctor told me to contact her anytime if I'm worried about anything."

"A doctor encouraging you to call? Nice."

"I know." I smiled. "Trauma has its rewards."

Down below a family strolled by, a perfect-looking couple walking their perfect-looking children along the perfect tree-lined Cambridge street. Slim with chestnut brown tresses effortlessly tied in a knot at the nape of her neck, the mom pushed a stroller. A toddler inside bounced his feet up and down and banged his hands on the bar, gabbing in garbled toddler talk. The dad wore Birkenstocks and had rumpled hair. He held an infant in a Snuggly across his chest, one hand caressing the baby's cheek while the other held a leash. These people even had a perfect yellow lab trotting along beside them.

"I hate them," I said to Leslie, gesturing with my eyes to the scene below.

"Me too."

We clinked our glasses in a toast as the family turned the corner. It would take several years before I no longer saw scenes of happy domesticity as symbols of my personal failing.

Leslie's Cambridge apartment was my home base throughout my stay, and I came and went, meeting other friends or just walking around the city. I'd always loved the neighborhoods surrounding Harvard Square. One afternoon I emerged from the subway into the heart of this bustling district of Cambridge, eager to spend the day on my own visiting my favorite bookstore, cafe, and park. I even planned to poke my head into the restaurant where I'd waitressed in my twenties, not that I'd know anyone anymore. But I wanted to breathe in the aroma of the enchiladas and burritos and fajitas, as if their scent would transport me to that carefree time in my life.

The jolt I felt in wandering the streets wasn't from joy. The cityscape looked the same: the buildings, the throng of people crowding the newsstand, the flow of the Charles River separating

Cambridge from Boston. But it all felt different. Walking through a busy city neighborhood is like a dance, stepping in time to the rhythm created by the mix of people, buildings, and traffic. I'd always easily picked up on and jumped into the cadence of a new environment. But here, in the very place I'd once lived and loved, I couldn't find the beat. I bumped into people repeatedly, and rather than being energized by the city's vibrancy, I felt enervated. Cambridge is made up of academics, artists, liberals, and small business owners—the sort of people I had always liked. So why did I feel I was in a Plexiglas bubble of isolation as I walked among them? I looked provincial in my cotton floral dress and worn sandals; even the Cambridge hippies looked more put together.

I sought refuge in a cafe, and the barista who rang up my order outed me.

"And where are you visiting us from, ma'am?"

I may as well have said Jupiter.

"I used to live here," I almost apologized, "but I live in North Carolina now. It's great to be back."

But as I sat at a small sidewalk table sipping decaf, I felt the same dull ache that shrouded me in Chapel Hill. I was still in a bad relationship, still pregnant, and still dreaming of Carly.

Another day I ate lunch with an old friend at a chic restaurant near Boston's Public Garden. Tricia and I had become friends a lifetime earlier when we were fresh out of college; fast-forward fifteen years, and our lives couldn't be more different. Tricia, in her Neiman Marcus office attire, blended in perfectly with the other patrons and developed an instant banter with the young, lithe waiter. He was enamored of her flirtatious smile and took no notice of me. I didn't blame him. I used to excel at repartee, but my mind felt sluggish. I remained mute while the two fired off one-liners.

As we ate overpriced Caesar salads amid the buzz of the crowd, Tricia asked how I was coping.

"Okay, I guess," I said.

"My mother had three miscarriages. Did I ever tell you this? No time to dwell on them with her other children needing attention. Maybe it was easier that way."

"Wow—didn't know that about your mother."

But guess what, I seethed inwardly, *a miscarriage is not the same as a stillbirth.*

Instead of telling Tricia about my incessant journal writing, or how I worried I was about being pregnant again, or how Jason and I were in serious trouble, I changed the subject.

"Catch me up on Frances."

And for the rest of our meal we stayed on the benign and safe terrain of a mutual friend.

Tricia wished me a safe trip back to Chapel Hill, and I felt a sting watching her red leather Coach bag swing from her shoulder as she melded into the busy street. Though never best friends, I knew in that moment our friendship was over.

At a dinner out with a couple of teacher buddies, I could tell they purposely avoided the subject of their children and husbands, likely a gesture of kindness. So we talked about teaching. My contributions were meager, as I'd left the school and the profession two years earlier, though reminiscing was fun. We idled in the parking lot after our meal and embraced tightly, but I couldn't help but fear our bond might weaken.

What would hold us together?

What would hold me to Boston anymore?

I took myself for a walk through the winding streets of Cambridge on a cool, sunny morning. I admired the rows of three-story, colorful Victorian houses and remembered how I used to wish I could afford such luxury and style. Now they seemed far too large and impractical. Feelings of loss followed me as the connection to the place I'd called home for a decade seemed to fray.

Soon my pregnant self would return to Chapel Hill, which still didn't feel like home. And I'd be back in a small house that wasn't nearly big enough to hold Jason and me and our collective unease.

⁓

Leslie and I settled into her balcony wicker chairs on my last night. Chirping crickets mixed in with the *whooshing* sounds of cyclists zipping down her street and dogs barking at a nearby park. A pair of citronella candles flickered on the small table between us.

"I'm nervous about going home tomorrow," I told Leslie. "No more getaways; just Jason and me."

"Do you think you'll get back on the same page?" Leslie asked, swatting away a mosquito. She knew that Jason and I needed a minor miracle to survive as a couple.

My knees were drawn into my chest, my arms wrapped around them.

"A lot needs to change for me to trust him again." I unwrapped my limbs and stretched my legs. "But, I'm pregnant," I said, laying a hand on my belly.

"You'll be okay," Leslie said, "no matter what." And her warm smile conveyed empathy, acceptance, and love. Just what I needed to ready myself for my return to North Carolina. Some friendships last a lifetime, and when Leslie and I hugged good-bye the next day, I knew ours would.

⁓

Fog enveloped the small airplane I was strapped into, and I couldn't see a single thing out my window. Jason and I had exchanged only a few clipped conversations while I was gone, nothing more than check-ins regarding my cats, the weather, the mail. Before boarding, I had called to remind him of my flight's arrival.

"Can you still pick me up?" I'd asked.

"Of course," he said, indignant, as if my question insulted him and his obvious role as my boyfriend. "How else would you get home?"

"I don't know. Sorry. I was just double-checking."

"It comes in at three?"

"Yeah. Don't bother parking. I'll meet you at the curb."

"Fine. See you soon."

I'd closed my eyes when I hung up. I pictured myself back in my little house, Jason's dirty work boots sitting by the back door, dishes no doubt piled in the sink, his anger oozing everywhere. I already felt stifled.

The plane hummed raucously. I rested my head in one hand, eating pretzels with the other and wondering if I'd eaten well enough during the trip. Trying to think like a pregnant woman, I'd once again given up caffeine and tried to eat plenty of protein. But these gestures at prenatal self-care were almost afterthoughts. I still hadn't connected to this baby. "Are you okay?" I whispered as the plane jetted through the skies. I gently tickled the skin around my naval and tried to picture a two-inch fetus floating just below my hand.

The flight attendant came through the aisle collecting trash.

"Tray tables up and seats forward, please," the pilot's voice crackled through the cabin. "We'll be on the ground shortly."

I obliged, closed my eyes, and braced myself for my least favorite part of flying. If there was ever a time I wanted a smooth landing, it was now.

Chapter 32—SPOT

~~~~~~

I stepped into the women's room before weaving through the crowded terminal. Two years earlier, when I'd first met Jason and flown to North Carolina for a visit, I'd done the same thing. That time I had reapplied lipstick and brushed my hair. Now I just wanted to pee.

I shoved my suitcase into the stall. My bladder emptied while I stared at the gray door and imagined the drive home from the airport. What would Jason and I talk about? Maybe I'd ask about my cats, maybe he'd ask about the flight. We wouldn't talk about Boston. As I unrolled a hunk of toilet paper, my gazed turned to my sky-blue panties. And then my eyes fixed on a brick-red spot of blood.

"What?" I whispered. "Shit." I wadded a ball of toilet paper on the stain and quickly left.

I sat alone on a bench outside the terminal, watching people embrace each other as they said hello and good-bye in front of idling cars. My mind raced: *What's happening? Am I just spotting? Or am I imagining things? Spotting sometimes happens. That's all this is. Every pregnancy is different, right?*

Pulling on the hem of my skirt to shield my knees from the hot sun, I noticed wisps of blonde hairs. Running my hand down my calf, I felt soft stubble beneath my fingertips. Another day without shaving. I felt not a single cramp or sensed any bleeding, but I couldn't move myself off the bench or even adjust my stance. Whatever my body was doing, better to stay put.

Jason was over fifteen minutes late. Really? He couldn't show up on time? At last I heard the familiar sound of a diesel engine chugging toward me. Not Jason, but a big, black truck. Four people spilled out, laughing and unloading luggage from the bed. Where was he? Even though I knew Jason would be angry if I called, I pulled out my cell phone.

"I'm almost there," his voice snapped after the second ring. "Five more minutes," and he hung up.

"Take your time," I muttered. "Me, my suitcase, and the spot on my panties will just roast in the heat."

A yellow taxi pulled up. I looked beyond it, hoping that Jason would be in the oncoming batch of cars. The back door of the taxi opened, and I recognized first Jason's foot in a black flip-flop, then his faded denim shorts and then his black T-shirt, then his drawn face, partly hidden beneath his orange cap. He walked slowly toward me, hands in his pockets.

"The truck won't start," he said.

"What?"

"I made it halfway to the airport, stopped for gas, and it wouldn't start."

"Where is it?"

"Near the mall. Let's go, the meter's running."

Jason took my suitcase, and I followed him into the backseat of the cab.

"Where to?" the driver asked.

"Back to my truck," Jason answered.

We drove in silence. Jason knew I'd be annoyed. I'd hated his truck from the minute he'd bought the thing sight unseen from a friend. Almost as soon as he'd driven the gas-guzzler home, the troubles started. Instead of confronting the friend or taking the truck to a mechanic, Jason tinkered on his own when the engine wouldn't start. When all else failed and he was stranded somewhere, he'd call me for a ride.

Once the cab merged onto the highway, Jason put his hand on my knee.

"How was the flight?"

"Fine," I answered, staring at the back of the driver's head. "I think I'm spotting."

I could feel his eyes on me.

"What?" His voice lowered.

I turned and looked at him. "Do I really need to say it again?"

Jason patted my knee and let out a long, slow sigh. "When did it start?"

"Just noticed it when I got off the plane." Pine trees whizzed by as the cab cruised down the highway.

His fingers tapped on my knee. "What does this mean?"

"I don't know. Maybe nothing. Maybe something's wrong."

Jason returned his hand to his lap.

The cab pulled into the gas station. "I'll be right back," Jason said. "Hopefully she'll start up."

He jogged toward his truck at the side of the building, keys dangling in his hand. I studied his profile while he finagled with the ignition, engine sputtering a few times before turning over for good. Jason's mouth formed a relieved smile.

"We're set," Jason said to the driver. "What do I owe you?"

"Twenty-five dollars," I heard the cabbie say as I climbed out with my suitcase. Jason followed behind, offering a hand for the large step up and into his truck. The heat was stifling, and the back of my thighs and calves burned as they settled into the seat. I found an old map to sit on, sparing my legs from the scalding and torn black Naugahyde.

"Hey, Kris," Jason said quietly, standing in front of my open door. "Do you have twenty dollars? For the driver?" His eyes darted back and forth, scanning my face for a reaction. "I only have ten."

Without answering or even looking at him, I pulled a few bills out of my wallet.

He leaned in closer. "I didn't think we'd need cash for cab fare, or I would have stopped at the bank. Sorry."

Chapter 33—DOOMED

A call to my new ob-gyn practice was all it took to land a same-day appointment.

The waiting room overlooked an atrium and the main hospital entrance. Voices, elevator chimes, and announcements from the P.A. drifted up to where Jason and I sat.

"You okay?" he periodically asked.

"Yeah. Just want this over with."

I'd awoken that morning with continued spotting, but not a cramp or even the slightest discomfort. I'd wanted to stay home. I did not want to be back in that place where life-altering news was doled out like Tylenol. I wanted no conversation with doctors or nurses puzzling through my unpromising symptoms. And I wanted nothing to do with an exam. What I did want was to find a good drug, numb out, and stay in bed.

A slight, middle-aged nurse practitioner with dark circles under her eyes finally took us to an examination room. She moved and talked slowly.

"Dr. Carter's in surgery and asked me to step in."

And then the litany of questions: "When was your last period? When did the spotting start? Are you having cramps?"

She jotted notes on her clipboard without glancing up or changing her expression. "Any other pregnancies?" she asked.

Was she kidding me? My record wasn't clearly marked?

"Yes, I had a baby six months ago. She was stillborn." *My apologies, Carly, for those prosaic words that diminish you.*

The nurse stopped writing and looked up. "Sorry," she whispered, almost frowned, and looked back down at her clipboard, clicking the pen cap open and shut with her thumb a couple of times before returning to her notes.

I wished Dr. Carter had been available. Even though I'd only met her once, at least she knew my history. I grew to hate saying "stillborn" to the unsuspecting; a lifetime of similar awkward moments, I realized, awaited me.

"Let's do an ultrasound and see what's going on," she said, standing up and pulling a machine next to the examination table. "Take off your clothes, put on this robe, and I'll be right back."

I wasn't panicky, nor did I replay my last ultrasound, the one that had showed Carly and her heart as still as stone. Teeth gritted and eyes shut, I only waited for the nurse to start the procedure so she could finish and I could go home. I never looked at the nurse or at Jason across the room. And I certainly did not look at the machine about to report the status of my teeny baby.

I would develop an aversion to exams and test results that revealed the inner workings of my body. Fifteen years later, I look at the ceiling during dental exams, never at the X-rays of my teeth hanging on the wall. I close my eyes during mammograms. When my bone density scans arrive in the mail, I cover the grainy picture and focus on the charts, tables, and graphs instead. I hold my breath until I get to the end of lab reports, exhaling only after I'm sure I haven't read the words "abnormal" or "positive."

In order to get a good picture of a thirteen-week fetus, an internal ultrasound is protocol. Which was like every other gynecological exam I'd ever had, except with live video feed broadcasting the latest misworkings of my uterus. The nurse asked if my dates might be off, as the fetus looked too small. Had she announced there was no heartbeat? Had she actually declared that the pregnancy was not viable? Had Jason walked across the room to see a picture of the fetus that had stopped growing? Or was the nurse the only one to bear witness to the small being, the second life that had come from Jason and me, the second one who wouldn't survive?

I don't remember how I came to learn what I already knew: that this baby, this pregnancy, was doomed.

The nurse talked to us in her office after I'd dressed. The weight of my purse felt good in my lap, and I ran my fingernail along the zipper while she discussed next steps. I opted against returning to the hospital for a D and C; I wanted to go home and stay there. Forever. With my broken body that simply refused to give life.

I let Jason hold my hand when the nurse explained what to expect with the miscarriage, when I should call a doctor, and how much ibuprofen to take.

"When the hard part is over," the nurse continued slowly, "you'll bleed for another few days until it eventually turns to spotting."

I focused on the soft *tick tick tick* sound my fingernail made on the zipper, and then finally asked, "So, should I expect something like a long, hard period?"

"Kind of. Your cramps may be relentless for a couple of hours. Take the ibuprofen. And schedule a follow-up visit in two weeks."

She stood up, and Jason and I followed her lead.

"Take care," the nurse said as she reached for the door handle, "and call if you have questions."

While I adjusted my purse strap along my shoulder, she slowly turned around, put both arms around me in a loose hug, and whispered in my ear, "I'm so sorry." The citrus scent of her shampoo and a close-up of her crow's feet startled me. I had no time to respond or hug her back before she dropped her arms and quickly stepped out the door.

And for the second time in six months, Jason and I left the same hospital with news of another failed pregnancy.

Chapter 34—Bed

The next morning brought increased spotting. How long would I have to wait for this miscarriage to be over? Jason had already left for a carpentry job, so it was just my cats and me. Exactly what I wanted. After breakfast, I sat myself on the sofa with a glass of water and barely read the opening pages of *The Da Vinci Code* when I felt cramping. My palm against my belly, I read a few more paragraphs. Within minutes, the spasms intensified as if a steel vise had begun clamping down on my insides.

For the next few hours, stabbing pain kept me balled up on the couch and sent me staggering to the bathroom as the failed life worked its way out. This was nothing like a hard period, rendering Ibuprofen as effective as baby aspirin. Moments of sweaty terror shot through me as the powerful cramps pierced and then ebbed. Was this much pain normal? Should I call someone? But the gut-twisting contractions left me unable to do anything: no reading or watching television or feeling sorry for myself or mustering up the thinking to pick up the phone.

I simply waited for the end.

It came several hours later, right around the time Jason pushed through the back door. As the pressure in my uterus subsided, I took note of the dampness covering my forehead and pooling in my armpits. My cats curled together in the yellow chair across the room, breathing in tandem, eyes squeezed shut, relaxed and peaceful as if nothing out of the ordinary had just happened. My legs felt constricted from my wrinkled capris tangled around my thighs. Jason's voice came from the kitchen.

"Are you okay?"

I glanced at the *The DaVinci Code* on the coffee table, still opened to the second page.

"I think so," I answered, straightening my shirt and untwisting my pants.

Jason sat next to me on the couch and put an arm around my shoulder while I propped my head against his chest. My body felt like a wrung-out, limp rag; my throat was dry.

"Can you hand me my water?" It was no longer cold, but I soaked up each tepid ounce. "And the ibuprofen."

My body came back to life with a slice of toast and a shower. I napped the rest of the afternoon, slept through the night, and didn't awaken until after Jason had left the next day.

Bright morning sun streamed into my kitchen while I waited for the kettle to boil. The light seemed falsely cheery, so I returned to the bedroom and retreated under the covers.

Sipping my Earl Grey tea, I saw my journal on the bedside table.

I opened to a blank page.

I miscarried.

I half expected my journal to jump in shock.

Did you hear this? My life-rejecting body lost another baby.

I put the journal down and stared at the ceiling. What was left to write that I hadn't written before: That I felt like a failure? That I was in a relationship on life support? That I would never be a mother? That I was approaching forty without feeling like I'd succeeded at anything?

I turned on the bedroom television to find Oprah, the self-help queen living her best life and dragging everybody up with her. "Go away," I said and turned to an episode of *Law and Order*. A pathological killer, I could stomach.

I stayed in bed, occasionally fetching a peanut butter sandwich or a handful of corn chips. I examined my face in the bathroom mirror. My straight hair looked drab and flat and limp, and the shadows under my eyes made my normally olive skin pale. I reached into the medicine cabinet and rubbed a dab of Vaseline on my dry lips and then squirted a dollop of hand cream into my palms. As I smoothed it in, I looked into my eyes. "You're old," I said, "you blew your youth, and now you're just old and wounded and dull."

Jason came home to find me in bed, in my pajamas, book in hand. He stood at the end of the bed, truck keys looped through his finger, a film of dirty sweat covering his arms.

"What are you doing?"

"Reading."

"Why are you in bed?"

"I don't know. Just feel like it, I guess."

"Have you eaten? Do you want dinner?"

He heated up a couple of cans of soup. We sat together on the deck, and I asked Jason about his job but didn't listen to his answer. He asked how I felt. I told him I was too tired to talk.

The next morning brought the same sad mood. Small streams flowed from my eyes and nose, down my neck, and onto my pillow.

Jason called from his job in the middle of the day.

"Why don't you go for a walk?" he suggested when I told him I was still in bed. "Or call your brother. Or mother."

"I'm still bleeding, you know. I don't want to go out."

"Sorry," Jason said. "I'm trying to help. I'll be home later."

Carly's photo was on the bedside table, and I looked at her forever-sleeping face.

I miss Carly more than ever, I wrote in my journal. *And I guess I should be mad at God or Bad Luck or something.*

My cats jumped on the bed and sniffed my face. *You smell the same*, they probably thought, *so why are you acting so strange?*

I wandered my house. Fed the cats and scooped their litter box. Took a brief shower. Refilled my water glass. Stood in front of the living room window and watched squirrels jump from branch to branch. The mailman emerged from the end of the street and made his way to the bottom of my driveway. He sorted through his bag for several minutes before stuffing my mailbox.

"Go get your mail," I whispered, standing at the threshold of my front door, breathing in fresh air for the first time in days. I knew I'd find only bills, catalogues, and circulars, so I stayed inside and continued to drift aimlessly as if on an ice floe.

Finally, a life preserver appeared. My nephew showed up at my back door and handed me a dogwood blossom.

"This is for you," he said.

"Oh, thanks." I took the pink sprig. "Do you want to come in?"

He kicked off his dirty flip-flops and sat his nine-year-old self on my sofa, colt-like legs folded underneath him. I offered him a glass of orange juice.

"How was the trip?" I asked, running my fingers through my unkempt hair, remembering that he had been invited to a friend's beach house. It was his first week ever away from his parents. His brown hair was highlighted from the sun, and a new patch of teeny freckles covered his nose and cheeks.

He told me about boogie boarding in the surf, and how he played cards at night, and how he still had leftover spending money because he didn't want to waste it all at the gift shop. His eyes were animated and happy, and his whole unmarred life lay ahead of him. I wanted to slip into his skin and be him for a day. Or an hour, which is how long he stayed and how long before I felt the muscles of my mouth smile and heard myself giggle when he stood with bent knees showing me how to boogie-board.

"I better go home," he finally said. "I told my Dad I'd clean my room before dinner. All the beach stuff is in a big pile on the floor."

We hugged good-bye, his skinny arms pressing against my back. "I'm glad you had fun," I told him, and watched him run through my yard and across the street to his house.

Turning on the water as hot as I could bear, I undressed and stepped into my second shower of the day. This time I stayed. My fingers massaged lavender-smelling shampoo into my scalp, and I inhaled the scented, steamy air. Next, I ran a loofah sponge across my arms and legs, back and belly, and imagined dead skin falling off, skimming past my feet before gliding down the drain. When there was nothing left to clean, I let the warm water stream down my back until my fingertips wrinkled and the hot water finally gave way to cold.

I covered my freshly cleaned self in a bathrobe and surveyed my bedroom: empty water glass, empty box of crackers, used Kleenex overflowing from the wicker trash bin. My journal sat beside Carly's photo, and I wondered if she'd watched as her wreck of a mother spent the last two days marooned in bed. I stripped the sheets, threw them in the wash, and drank a glass of water outside on the deck. The late-day temperature was hot, and I scooted my chair into the shade of a pine tree's big, soft branches. I was within arms' reach of the cherry tomato plant I'd started in the spring, and popped a bright red one into my mouth, closed my eyes, and felt the warm, sweet juices and slick seeds against my tongue. I savored the soft flesh, eyeing the remaining ripe tomatoes on the vine. Ten in all. Should I put them in a salad, a real meal tonight? Save some for Jason?

I relaxed back in the chair, watched a pair of cardinals dive in and out of the trees, and one by one, ate them all.

Chapter 35—DONE

~~~~~

Nobody mourned the miscarriage. Friends said things like, "Well, the timing would have been hard for another baby" or "Your body had hardly recovered from Carly." Or my favorite, "Your miscarriage was a blessing in disguise."

I didn't feel blessed.

Thoughts about God and injustice began to show up in my journal. My belief in a God was unformed; at best it was an idea to explore. I was more comfortable pondering mystery, like an angel image appearing on my computer screen. I wondered about an afterlife, and the nature of an unseen spiritual world where I hoped Carly dwelled. But God as the Master Planner? The Decision Maker? The Captain at the Helm of Everything? I wasn't sure.

If I choose to believe in God, I wrote in my journal, *He is either punishing or indifferent. If He has the power to dole out blessings and good fortune and sacred little beings who need shepherding into adulthood, why am I off the list? How omniscient is He? Can't He see I would have been a good mother?*

A few friends suggested I get angry with God, but I didn't want to. Maybe I would make an angry God angrier or a benevolent God turn on me because I was focusing on my losses instead of looking around and seeing that everyone hurt and why not count the obvious blessings in my life.

God, I wrote, *has a lousy job description. Maybe it is simple accounting, having to giveth and taketh away even if He'd rather not.*

Babies or no babies, the world outside beckoned. I had to buy food and toothpaste and stamps and keep my life going. One afternoon while unloading groceries, I thrust aside Jason's unopened mail strewn about the kitchen counter. It landed in a jumbled mess across the floor, and as I looked at the pile, I thought of Jason and me. We were also a jumbled mess. I couldn't delay the inevitable any longer. Our relationship was destroyed. We had nothing for each other. We were done.

Still, my voice shook when that evening I told him I wanted to separate.

"Too much has happened," I said, sitting on the edge of the bed. "We haven't been good for a long time. We don't belong together."

Jason looked as if what I'd told him was outlandish, as if I were leaving him to join the army. His eye searched mine with creased brows, his mouth agape.

"Well, I still love you." His words sounded like a question, as if for the first time he wondered aloud about his feelings.

"We fight too much."

"Couples fight."

"Not like us. Besides, I need to get back on my feet. Without you. I need to fix myself."

Jason sat next to me and reached for my hand. His skin was bronzed from sun, sweat, and dirt, and his body still radiated heat from the sizzling summer day.

"I don't want to give up," he said. "We've had a hard year. Actually, I was thinking I'd go to Europe in September."

Huh? I turned to face him.

Jason had a scheme of touring sustainably built buildings in France and Germany. And when I asked him what a possible trip had to do with us, he explained that it would give us space and a chance for a fresh start when he returned.

Had we been in two different relationships?

"Well, travels or not," I finally said, "I can't go on like this. Let's talk more about this soon."

I'd lived with Jason long enough to question how he'd manifest a trip to Europe; what about his mountain of debt? But I'd planted the seed of separation, and if the notion of a trip helped him view September, a mere six weeks away, as a target exit date from the house, so be it.

I began anticipating a future without Jason, whether or not he was ready to believe it. I knew my salary would not adequately support my living solo in the house, so one week later, I interviewed for a position teaching remedial English two evenings a week at a nearby community college. The additional income would provide the cushion I'd need, and I signed a contract on the spot.

My mood lifted as I planned for my class and imagined teaching again. I wondered what it would be like to have adult students instead of children. I also wondered how I'd juggle two jobs. My new teaching position would start the same week I'd return to my three-quarter position at the university, putting an end to my unstructured summer days. Rather than fret about the rest of my life, I'd worry about when I'd eat dinner the nights I taught, and how to sustain my energy working an additional job.

I began to mentally claim the house as my own. I imagined peace and solitude, reconnecting with myself, bonding with Carly free from distractions. I bought a wall hanging, squares of various shades of blue stitched together with tiny sequins scattered about. This would hang over the bed once Jason was gone, adding richness and warmth to the otherwise white walls. I bought sheer, sage-green curtains with embroidered leaves to soften the stark expanse of the living room's sliding glass doors. I tacked inspirational mementos to a small bulletin board: the printout of the angel's image I'd discovered on my computer, the Ram Dass letter Jennifer had sent, a greeting card with a hopeful verse by Rumi written in loopy script letters beneath a vibrant purple and yellow iris:

> *"This is the way you slip through into your innermost home: Close your eyes and surrender."*

I wanted this. Wanted to return to my Self, to find sanctuary. My bulletin board would hang near my rocking chair in the bedroom, and this little nook would be where I'd read, journal, and heal. I could hardly wait to clear the house of all its misery and rechristen it as the place where I'd become whole again.

Jason never saw my purchases, as I kept them hidden and kept myself scarce. When he was home, I looked for excuses to leave. I went to the movies, read home improvement magazines in the Barnes and Noble cafe, took long, ambling walks after dinner, returning as nightfall finally consumed the last sliver of light. Jason grew petulant as my absences increased. He'd leave his grimy work boots in the house, pieces of dirt fallen in a circle around them. His contribution to the kitchen was to stack his dirty dishes in the sink. His truck continued to strand him and he'd routinely call for rides. No apology, no promise to get it fixed, just a curt, "I'm at the Exxon station" or "I'm on the shoulder of the road near the big church." If I refused to pick him up, I knew Jason would let loose anger, so it was easier to stop cooking or reading or whatever I was doing, retrieve him, and silently count the days until he and his truck were no longer my responsibility.

On the eve of the 2004 Summer Olympics opening ceremonies, Jason found me stretched on the sofa with textbooks, folders, and pens, finalizing the syllabus for the class I'd start teaching.

"I'm excited for you," Jason said, standing against the doorframe. "It'll be fun for you to be in the classroom again."

"Yeah, I think so," I said, putting my pencil down and sitting up. "Jason, we need to finish talking about separating."

"You mean talking about how you are giving up?"

His cautiously friendly expression quickly turned pouty, mouth downturned and tight.

"Come on."

"But it's what you're doing."

"I'm trying to help us. Both of us."

"Quitting isn't helping."

"Jason, are you really happy the way things are?"

He stared blankly at the faded carpet. Shifting his weight from one foot to the other, he finally looked at me. Our eyes locked.

"Honestly, Kris, part of our difficulty is *you*. *I* need to have some fun. I know things haven't been easy for you, but I'm tired of being cooped up in this house. Tired of supporting you."

I felt my face heat up and blush.

"What kind of support do you think you've been giving?"

"Emotional," Jason sighed. "We don't stand a chance with your brooding apathy. I'm drained."

Anger swirled inside of me like a growing hurricane. My fists clenched as I resisted the sudden urge to charge Jason. Electric jolts seemed to shoot through my arms and legs, and every cell in my body felt on edge. This surge of energy unnerved me, like I was on a roller coaster about to careen down a hill with no brakes.

"You've been *supporting me*?" I practically snorted in disgust. "What a *joke*."

Jason stood taller at the sound of my loud voice, legs planted wide as if preparing himself for battle.

"You've been *angry* with me!" I fumed. "And for *what*?"

I slammed my book on the coffee table. Then I picked it up again and threw it across the room. Magazines and a couple of coasters lay innocently on the table, and with a sweep of my arm, I sent them flying.

"Asshole," I snarled.

I bounded past Jason into the bedroom. He followed.

"You know what your problem is?" he hissed slowly from the doorway, chest thrust out and nostrils flared. "You're snooty. Another goddam snooty northerner."

His voice grew louder with each word until finally spittle had gathered in the corners of his mouth. He spun around and marched across the hall to his office, banging the door shut behind him.

Sweat formed on my upper lip as heat flushed through my body and the sound of blood rushed through my ears. My lungs heaved as if I'd sprinted around a track. With no thought, I grabbed the bedroom door and slammed it shut. Then I opened and slammed it again, this time harder. And then I did it again. And again. How many slams did it take before a chunk of wood from the doorjamb chipped off and fell at my feet?

Silence.

My hands and limbs felt rubbery; the house almost reverberated. The months of strain and grief and anger and longing had become too much for our once beloved nest, and it seemed to vibrate disapproval. Each room, each wall, each fixture had tired of Jason and me, and the slice of doorjamb on the floor served as notice:

"Keep this up," the small ranch warned, "and I will fall down around you."

I imagined first one wall cracking, then another crumpling, and then the roof caving, leaving nothing but a heap of debris, covering all traces of Jason and me and our train-wrecked lives.

I lay on the bed with the palms of my hands resting on my belly, and stared at the spinning ceiling fan until my breath slowed. Hypnotized by the whirring blades, my body gradually calmed; I shut out the light and fell asleep.

In the morning there was no sign that Jason had slept next to me. I quickly packed a bag with my journal and textbooks, loaded up the cats' dishes with food and water, tiptoed out of the house, and backed my car slowly down our gravel driveway. A wedge of the sun was surfacing on the honey-tinged horizon.

In a coffee shop, I sipped a latte at a corner table and watched as the place came to life. A sleepy-looking barista with a thick mop of untamed hair, stubbly beard, and wire-rimmed glasses greeted the slow but growing stream of caffeine-craving customers. Some had freshly coiffed hair and lipstick and some wore business suits, but all dashed in and out quickly, car keys jangling in their impatient hands, anxious to get going.

Explosion, I wrote in my journal. *Boom. Crash. Burn. We are over. Beyond over. Nothing left but ashes. I can't wait to be alone.*

Later in the morning I sank into a soft chair in the public library and read the newspaper. I browsed through new releases in fiction. I stared through the tall windows into the woods that abutted the library. My body felt calm and serene, as if last night's eruption had either never happened or had released every last ache and pain. Surrounded by books and kindly librarians and senior citizens, my thoughts were clear, and for the first time in ages, I felt like I was behind the wheel of my life. Sure, I didn't know where I was headed, but I was driving.

In the afternoon, I went to a matinee and immersed myself in a murder mystery and warm, salty popcorn. I took myself for tacos at a Mexican cafe, and then bought a new blouse at Macy's. One more small charge on my Visa would not break my bank, I reasoned; I was about to earn extra income, after all.

As the day ended, I pulled into my driveway and walked through the front door to find Jason in the kitchen dumping a can of corn chowder into a pot. He didn't look up. I sat at the kitchen table while he slowly stirred a wooden spoon through the soup, his back to me.

"It's over, Jason."

He poured the chowder into a bowl, leaned against the stove, and began eating.

"Let's put an end to our misery."

His spoon clanked against the bowl between slurps.

"Will two weeks be enough time for you to find a place to stay?"

Jason gave no sign that he was listening, just kept sipping his soup. I stared at him, curious. Would he say *anything*?

"Kris," he finally spoke in a hushed, monotone voice. "Okay. I'll go."

And then he finished eating, placed the bowl in the sink, and left the house.

My two cats jumped into my lap, pushing their heads into my hands, demanding to be stroked. They walked back and forth across my legs, purring loudly as if to claim me for themselves. Or to voice their joy at my return, or to lodge their complaint that I'd left them again.

"I'm not going away anymore," I whispered. "It's just the three of us from now on." Closing my eyes, I pictured Carly's sleeping face in the photo. "And you too, little girl."

Chapter 36—TRUCK

I helped Jason pack, not because I was feeling kind and generous, but because he hadn't procured a single box, much less filled one. He'd found a room to rent four miles away, and days before he was due to leave, I tracked down packing supplies, helped him inventory his belongings, even wrote out a grocery list when he asked what I thought he should buy. I filled large trash bags with his clothes, bedding, towels, and stuffed boxes with CDs, books, and desk supplies.

On moving day, his truck wouldn't start. No surprise. What did surprise me, however, was my lack of anger and irritation that I'd need to drive him to his new place and arrange for him to get his truck later that week. A niggling of sadness also caught me off guard. What would happen to Jason? Could he support himself? We packed my car wordlessly.

"We don't have to do this, you know," he said as I started the engine. "This can just be for a few weeks, a month, until we can clear the air and start again."

He would have stayed if I'd let him, asking me more than once in the preceding week if I really wanted to go through with the separation.

"We better leave," I said, and his slow eye roll signaled his resignation that I wasn't changing my mind.

I never entered his new house but helped him unload my car while the engine was running. I asked Jason about the three sedans lined up along the side of his new driveway, and he told me that his landlord was the elderly homeowner who rented out all of her bedrooms. I pictured Jason cohabitating with assorted transients and a kind older woman playing the de facto matriarch of her makeshift family.

"Okay, that's everything," I said. Jason stood sullenly beside the pile in the driveway, his head down and hands in his pocket. Finally, he picked up a box with one hand and with the other heaved a bulging trash bag over his shoulder and walked into his new house.

Tears pooled in the corners of my eyes and spilled down my cheeks as I drove away. How had we lost so much so quickly?

I felt unsettled all afternoon. Concern and pity for Jason were mixed with relief that he was gone and gratitude that we'd gotten through the drop-off without drama. I tried napping, flipped through the newspaper, and walked around the block. Finally I called my brother.

At a noisy restaurant a few hours later with my brother and his family, I polished off a juicy cheeseburger, salty fries, and a Dos Equis.

"I think you'll be surprised how quickly you'll adjust," David said, "to being without Jason."

He joked with my nephew about how much homework he'd have once school started, and I joked that I'd pile the homework on to *my* students. I didn't expect to have fun on the very day Jason moved out and felt a pang of guilt. Jason, who'd only been gone for a few hours, would have felt hurt if he'd known my family was laughing together in a crowded burger joint, devouring fry after greasy fry and swigging the last gulps of our beers.

Though my single years in Boston seemed as far away as a dream, locking up my house and readying for bed on my own felt natural. My cats snuggled against me in bed, and all three of us slept soundly. When the morning sun filtered through the blinds, I massaged my cats' ears and looked around the room.

"Come on, boys," I said. "Let's get up."

I unearthed my new household purchases from the back of my closet and got started. Wall hanging finally secured over my bed and bulletin board beside my rocking chair, I sat down and took in the updated space.

"How do you like the wall hanging?" I asked my cats, who stood on their back legs and reached their front paws up the wall to touch and sniff. "Well, *I* like it."

I hung the gauzy green curtains in the living room and stood back to admire them. And then the doorbell rang.

"Shit." I assumed it was my brother. At nine in the morning? Why wouldn't he call first?

I glanced in the mirror on the way to the door and tightened my bathrobe belt. I opened the door a crack.

"Jason? What are you doing here?"

The puffy bags under his eyes and his downturned mouth gave away his temper. His face shone with perspiration, and grapefruit-sized sweat stains covered the armpits of his shirt.

"How did you get here?"

"I walked," Jason growled. "And I'm hungry. I've got a twin bed in a small room and that's where I stayed all of yesterday. I hate it there, and I want my truck."

Damn him, I thought. *He's going to make this hard every step of the way.*

Jason helped himself to a bowl of cereal and a cup of coffee, then puttered around the house checking drawers and closets for anything he might have forgotten. Without speaking, I thumbed through a magazine at the kitchen table, wondering if he'd noticed the new curtains. When he went outside to try his truck, I silently begged the entire universe to start the engine. Mercifully, I heard the familiar whirring. Leaving the truck running, Jason returned to the kitchen and planted himself squarely in front me to complain of the injustice that I got to stay in the house while he was stuck in a teeny room filled with strangers.

"You'll be fine," I said, certain my irritation was obvious. "It hasn't even been twenty-four hours. Go out and buy groceries while your truck is running, and then go back to the house and make conversation with whoever's around. Give this time."

"Fine," he grumbled. I peeked through a window and breathed relief as his maroon truck turned the corner and vanished.

Back to my solitude.

The rest of the day unfolded peacefully. I walked around the house and pictured myself going to bed each night alone, waking each morning alone. Being alone. I sat in my rocking chair and reread all the messages on my new bulletin board. I sampled the new sage curtains in different positions, tied back with a sash or hanging loosely on their own. After a midday outing to pick up groceries, I prepared a salmon steak with rice and salad for supper. The sound of a barking dog wafted through my kitchen's open windows as night fell. I stepped outside and listened. The sonorous bays were deep and suggested no hint of distress. This was a dog, I imagined, enjoying a summer evening. "Hello!" the dog's barks seemed to say to the glossy North Star and half-moon dangling overhead. "Hello!" he cried to the chattering katydids and cicadas. "I'm here!" he reveled to the leggy pines and sultry summer air. "I'm alive."

"Me too," I whispered, looking toward the shimmering stars.

Chapter 37—ALONE

F all semester underway, my days felt purposeful and busy in a way they hadn't since Carly died. There was plenty to do: prepare lesson plans for the classes I taught two evenings a week at the community college, work as a learning specialist at the university during the day, make lunches and dinners for my long nights, clean the house on the weekend. The pace buoyed me.

A few of my community college students were fresh out of high school, but many were single mothers no older than thirty, with some in their forties and fifties. Most were Latino or African American, and some newly graduated from a nearby drug rehabilitation program. I was the minority in many ways, probably for the first time in my life, and it struck me one night when I drove home that I felt like a minority in my personal life as well. I knew few women my age who were also unmarried and childless.

I was adapting to my new solitary routines of evening meals and weekends alone, but sharing aisles in the supermarket with mothers and their kids could still be tough. These family scenes not only triggered pangs about Carly's absence but now also reminded me of my uncertain future. *If I'm not going to have* that *life*, I wondered while watching women fill their carts, toddlers in tow chewing on animal crackers, *what life* will *I have*? On weekends I often walked through Chapel Hill's wooded trails. Passing pairs of slow-moving women laden with strollers and tales of potty training, I felt left out. Sometimes on a Football Saturday, a day when the entire town sprang to life to cheer on the university team, I'd stroll downtown amid the throngs of fans. Sounds of drunken revelry poured out of lively bars. Had that once been me in Boston? Carefree? Sipping a drink and laughing with friends? I missed the feeling of youthful innocence, though yearned for my Boston life less and less. What did I want now?

With less free time than ever, I still found time to dive into my journal. The blank pages held an invitation to my inner world, and sometimes seeing my journal on my bedside table brought a palpable sense of ease. When the day ahead felt too hectic, when I longed for a close friend to talk to, or when I was filled with worry that I'd mourn Carly forever, I knew relief awaited me in that eggplant-colored book.

> *Dear Carly,*
> *I expected to be lonely once Jason moved out, but I'm glad to be alone. What I didn't expect was to miss you even more than before. Sometimes you seem nearby. Other times you seem to slip further away. Where do you go?*

I'd told Jason he could keep some of his tools in the garage until he found storage, and he occasionally showed up at the house to grab a power saw or a sander or whatever else he needed for the short-term carpentry projects that continued to keep him afloat. I was in the yard, raking leaves into piles during one particular Saturday afternoon stop-by. After a pleasant hello, Jason reflected on what he thought had contributed to our demise.

"I needed a partner who believed in me and my business. You resented me."

I couldn't disagree with him, though I wasn't about to say so. I remember how Jason's enthusiasm and optimism had once seemed the perfect antidote to my unremitting practical approach to everything. Where I saw barriers, Jason only saw possibilities.

"Jason, you don't really want to talk about this, do you?"

"I am going to make it, Kris," he said as he turned to leave. "Just watch."

So I did. I watched him saunter to his truck and watched him drive away.

My fortieth birthday came and went with no big party, no "over-the-hill" jokes, no spa weekend with girlfriends, no trip to New York to see a show. None of my pre-Carly, pre–North Carolina fantasies about celebrating this landmark birthday played out. I went to the mountains with my family for a weekend. The serene surroundings and easy ambles around the small mountain town matched my state of being. All I'd wanted to do since Jason moved out was find my footing and a new normal; big festivities would have felt out of sync.

Dear Carly,
Your mother is now forty. Old! I'm missing you as I see the stores fill with Halloween costumes. You should see the elaborate getups some babies are forced to wear. I might have dressed you as a bunny in a brown jumper with felt ears and a fluffy cottontail. Nothing over the top. I hope you're okay, wherever you are. I try to keep you close, but also want you to be free. It's hard holding on and letting go.

On a teaching night while everybody in my class completed a reading assignment, I sat next to a student and helped her with verb conjugations.

"I work full time at Hardees," Kiana said, "and I barely have time for homework. I'm so tired, but I've got to pass my classes so I can get into the nursing program."

Kiana had just graduated from high school and looked every bit a teenager with her creamy, taut skin, large ebony eyes, narrow hips, and reed-like legs.

"That's great," I said. "Nursing is a good, steady field."

"I know. I need it." And she unbuttoned her sweater to show me her baby bump.

"Oh my goodness." I smiled. "Congratulations."

Kiana went on to tell me how she and her boyfriend lived separately at their respective mothers' homes, trying to save money to rent a place of their own. They fought a lot, and sometimes she thought she should just go it alone but needed his help with money. This not-quite-yet adult was forging ahead through an unforgiving schedule and circumstances, and I felt drained on her behalf. Then she told me her baby's due date. Carly's birthday.

"Wow," I said, my belly tightening into a knot, "you don't look that far along."

"I know. I'm small." Kiana giggled. "Just like you. Do you have any babies?"

"No. I don't," I said, wanting to disappear into the cinder block walls of the classroom.

Flattened, I drove home along the dark and nearly empty highway. "I'm sorry, Carly," I whispered, "but I didn't want to scare Kiana. You'll always be the center of my heart even if I don't tell everyone about you, okay?"

At home I stared at Carly's picture, hoping that I'd see her in a dream that night. Then I remembered a Rumi poem I'd copied into my journal months earlier and thumbed through the pages until I found it.

Your body is away from me
But there is a window open
from my heart to yours.
From this window, like the moon
I keep sending news secretly.

Turning to a new page, in loopy handwriting I wrote:

Carly, Carly, Carly, Carly, Carly.

CHAPTER 38—DEER

The uncertain view of my life ahead felt sometimes intol-
erable, and for a brief stint I considered adoption. *Why
not become a mother another way?* I thought, fantasizing
about bringing home an orphaned baby from China or East-
ern Europe. I'd have a purpose, a new identity, no longer the
Unmarried-Over-Forty-Woman-Who-Lost-a-Child. I'd be that
Cool-Woman-with-That-Cool-Kid-from-Kazakhstan. I'd arrange
playdates and birthday parties and would find time to volunteer at
the schools. I'd be with the Haves, not the Have-Nots.

Scouring the Internet, I became expert on the best agencies
for foreign adoptions. I spoke to a social worker, talked to adop-
tive mothers, and filled a notebook outlining steps to take on the
lengthy path to adoption. I wrote letters to friends detailing my
plans. But as I began to fully understand the grueling and expensive adoption process, not to mention the cost of raising a child
alone, I stumbled. I'd need a loan to afford the legal fees, and also
a better paying job. Pondering the mountain of logistics I'd have
to scale overwhelmed me.

One Friday after work, I walked several blocks through cold, pelting rain to collect my car. I'd sometimes leave it for the day at a small house-converted office building when I wanted a commute free of the restrictive bus schedule. The late afternoon October sun had already sunk, and streetlights illuminated the puddles. When I reached the house, a thick, steel chain blocked the entrance to the small gravel driveway where my Jetta sat alone.

"Everyone's gone? It's only five thirty," I said aloud. "What about my car?"

Each side of the chain was attached to a three-foot wooden post. A clump of chain was looped and wrapped and tied around one post, its tail nowhere to be seen.

I pulled at the knotty mass with both hands, trying to slip it off the post, but it was heavy and taut and wouldn't budge. Meanwhile, rain steadily soaked into my hair, my denim jacket, and my corduroys. Jimmying the umbrella between my neck and shoulder, I tried to create slack by pulling toward the center of the chain, managing to scrape my hands and nothing else.

"My car is trapped behind Fort Knox," I spewed. "Dammit!"

I threw my umbrella to the ground and crossed my arms. By now, small puddles had formed in the soles of my drenched clogs. Streams of rain flowed from my hair down my face and neck. I pictured my raincoat hanging in my closet at home.

A thick rusty nail was hammered through the center of one of the chain links into the post, its last inch bent toward the post and forming a triangle. Taking a pen from my backpack, I tried straightening the nail. Like a brittle twig, the pen snapped in half and I threw it next to the umbrella.

"*Shit*!" I yelled into the blowing rain.

"Did you try the other side?"

I turned toward the voice. An elderly woman with a large umbrella was walking by slowly, her silver curls peeking out beneath her rain hat.

"What?" I said, wiping the drops of mascara-tinted rain from my eyelashes.

"Try the other side."

Across the driveway, a shiny metal latch was screwed into the other post. The end of the chain was hooked neatly on the latch, and with my now raw fingers, I opened it easily.

"Oh my gosh, I can't believe it," I said, turning back to thank the woman, but she was gone.

In a steamy shower that night, I laughed aloud at the evening events. If that kind lady hadn't ambled by, I might have worked the chain on the wrong post until my fingers were nubs.

"Do I need a clearer sign?" I asked aloud as the warm water finally took the chill from my bones. "Adopting a baby? Alone? After everything that's happened? Ever consider walking the path of least resistance?"

I wrapped myself in the fluffy robe my mother had sent for my thirty-ninth birthday, set a simple table, and poured a glass of white wine. As spinach and potato soup simmered on the stove, I opened my journal.

Don't make your life any more complicated, I wrote. *Simplify. Have faith. Be patient.*

———◦———

"I'm going for a walk," I said to my cats one night after cleaning up dinner dishes. They looked up briefly from where they were snoozing on the sofa and closed their eyes again. Another quiet Saturday evening with nothing special to do. Weekends when I felt lonesome, I'd call a Boston friend, wondering if I'd ever find close girlfriends in Chapel Hill. Weekends when I enjoyed my solitude, I wondered what this might portend. Would I turn into a loner?

The autumn air was cool, and the clouds were tinted shades of orange against a dimly lit sky. Passing my neighborhood's humble ranch homes, I caught glimpses of domesticity through the windows: lively TV screens, a family sitting around a kitchen table, a grooming cat on a windowsill. I turned down a narrow unpaved street, gravel crunching under my tennis shoes. As I approached the end of the street, I stopped short at the sight of a large, antlered buck not more than twenty feet from me. He was grazing intently in a small yard, and in the shadows of pine trees behind him, I spotted four more deer. They chewed greens from large shrubs, appearing focused and relaxed, as if they'd found the perfect site for a late night snack. When a distant car's engine rumbled, the deer startled and looked up. They saw me, and all of us stood frozen, watching each other. I watched their soft ears twitching, studied the white markings circling their perfectly round eyes, and followed the rhythm of their rib cages expanding and contracting with each inhale and exhale.

I didn't know why, but an imperative to stay with the small brood took hold, and when a creamy-colored fawn stepped toward me, I eagerly held my breath. Would she come closer? Close enough so I could hear her breath, see her eyelashes, perhaps reach my hand to her face? Would she sniff my fingers and then let me stroke her silky ears? Would the rest of the deer let me sit on the grass while they nibbled and foraged around me? Could I spend the rest of the night right here, among these gentle creatures and the loblolly pines and the shard of moon hanging tenderly overhead?

I wanted to. I wanted the encounter to last. I continued to stand like a statue, and except for the few steps taken by the fawn, so did the rest of the deer. The wind whistled like a distant flute, gently shaking the pine needles overhead and blowing the yard's fallen leaves into a small eddy. The large buck turned to the adjacent grove of trees, looked back toward me, and then strode nimbly into the woods. The darling fawn, as if possessing springs instead of legs, leapt up and darted close behind. Within seconds, the rest of the pack skittered away, kicking up twigs and leaves as they dashed off, their bouncing white tails the last thing visible.

"Good night," I whispered.

The rapidly darkening sky turned the remaining clouds steely and black. Leaves rustled and swirled at my feet. Closing my eyes, I zipped up my sweatshirt and filled my lungs with the crisp air. Carly seemed near. I yearned for her, but amid the peaceful surroundings and my uncluttered mind, I ached less.

"Such a perfectly beautiful night," I sighed. "There's nowhere else I'd rather be than right here."

My step felt lighter as I made my way home.

Chapter 39—LAKE

～～～

I spent Thanksgiving at the farm, the same place I'd celebrated a year earlier. Only then I was thirty-five weeks pregnant and with Jason. We'd imagined that at our *next* Thanksgiving we'd be juggling a diaper bag, a squirmy ten-month-old, and cranberry sauce.

I drove my newly single self to the party. Half a dozen tables were set up outside, adorned with miniature pumpkins and gourds and small vases with orange mums. About thirty of us sat together under a warm November sun. I slipped my shoes off and burrowed my bare feet into the thick bed of soft grass while eating the requisite turkey, green bean casserole, and mashed potatoes. I was glad to be in a crowd and, despite my only casual relationships with the farm residents, surprised myself with my own joking and laughing.

After the midday feast, I left the mingling guests, walked to the end of the farm's main road, continued down a narrow path, and made my away across the large field of overgrown grass. There was the small magnolia tree Jason and I had planted for Carly at her memorial service. We'd visited it only once before our relationship free fall. The tree was taller, but not by much.

"Hi, Carly. It's me."

A trio of crows swooped across the field, their shrill *caaaaws* reverberating around me.

"Today is Thanksgiving, and it's almost your birthday."

I stood in front of the narrow trunk and waxy, olive leaves of Carly's tree and wondered how to mark the upcoming anniversary of her birth and death. Maybe I'd return to this very spot on her birthday? Maybe I'd plant something else? I trusted that an idea would come to me. As the sun lit up the fiery foliage lining the edges of the field, my heart softened with the thought of Carly's magnolia maturing and merging with the picturesque landscape.

Back at home, I changed into sweats and opened my journal.

Hi Carly—Did you see me navigating that party by myself? I'm not sure, but I may have been semi-charming and looked quasi-attractive. Or at least not so worn out. Progress! In the spirit of Thanksgiving, know that I'm so very grateful for your presence.

Grocery shopping on a busy Saturday, I ran into the father of a middle-school girl I'd once tutored.

"We're moving to Zambia for two years," Bill said, "and need to rent our basement apartment while we're gone. If you know of anyone who might be a good tenant, please give them my number."

"Will do. Sounds like you're off on an adventure."

We chatted briefly about his daughter, the travel perks of his wife's work, plans for Christmas. I'd always liked this family and provided tutoring right up until the end of my pregnancy. It wasn't until the next morning when I was busy with laundry and bills that it dawned on me. *I should rent that apartment.*

I'd never seen the basement, but the main house was lovely. The dining room, where I had re-taught algebra to Bill's spirited preteen, looked out over a generous, lush lawn with an elegant weeping willow in the middle. Azaleas, camellias, and hydrangeas nestled among the pines; irises, coneflowers, and daisies sprang up in patches. The backyard rolled gently to the edge of a lake, and while I'd wait for my tutee to finish working a problem, I'd gaze through a large picture window and watch the occasional gliding kayaker.

I called Bill to ask about the rent and grinned when he told me that he planned to charge three hundred dollars *less* than what I currently paid, but because he knew me, he'd reduce it by another hundred. Utilities included. This was all too good to believe. I'd be able to leave my teaching job at the end of the academic year. I imagined drinking my morning tea on the dock. I imagined being surrounded by flowers, coasting in a canoe.

Bill walked me through the apartment that very afternoon. Each room had expansive lake views, and the enormous kitchen came equipped with new appliances, new cabinets, and a huge, walk-in pantry. The front door opened to a brick patio bordering a row of rose bushes. A second patio facing a flower garden was accessed through a second bedroom. Tile floors throughout would feel cool during hot summers, and a gas fireplace in the living room would keep the winter chill at bay. Bill's sister-in-law, whom I'd met several times, would live in the main house upstairs, and I knew she would make a quiet yet friendly neighbor.

"I'll take it," I told Bill as we stood outside what would be my new front door. The December wind kicked up the lake and tiny waves crashed against the dock. Honking geese flew overhead.

"Super." He smiled. "It will be ready the second week in January. When can you move in?"

I pulled out my calendar and stared at the red heart I had drawn on January 14th. Carly's birthday fell on a Friday of a three-day weekend. The extra day to unpack and settle in before returning to work would be welcome.

I smiled and asked, "How about the fourteenth?"

I couldn't imagine a better way to mark Carly's birthday.

Chapter 40—NAMEPLATES

~~~~~~

And so I spent Carly's first birthday with a couple of movers and dozens of boxes. Jason called, and in a few short words—and in what would be our final conversation—we acknowledged the significance of the day. My brother and sister-in-law brought dinner, and we sat around my kitchen table, admiring the new cabinets, the teal walls, and the lake beyond the windows. Two thoughts vied for my attention: the unpacking that lay ahead and what this day *might* have looked like. Before falling asleep in my new bedroom, I pulled out my journal.

> *Happy Birthday to my One-Year-Old Girl. I miss you and wish you could be here eating your first-ever birth-day cake. You should see the beautiful house I moved into. You would love it. A great big lawn to run around on and a canoe to paddle up and down the lake. Geese and ducks even play by the dock. I've been so busy this week packing up, but you're always in my thoughts, especially today. I do have something special planned to honor you, but it will have to wait for a few more days.*

A week later, I drove several boxes of children's books to the local chapter of the Ronald McDonald house, a home-away-from-home for families with ill children. I'd been collecting favorite children's books from friends and family since the holidays, and used a computer publisher program to design bookplates. Three-inch square stickers edged with lavender scrolls surrounded the words "In Loving Memory of Carly." I'd amassed piles of books, including *The Polar Express*, *Fantastic Mr. Fox*, and *The Hungry Caterpillar*, and one by one had stuck a bookplate onto the inside cover of each.

"Hi there," I said to the cheery young woman at the front desk. "I'm here to donate books to your children's room."

"How nice." She smiled warmly. Her flaxen hair was tied back in a ponytail, freckles scattered across her nose, and her brick-red, fleece pullover was zipped up to her neck. "We so appreciate donations. You can leave the box with me and I'll get one of our volunteers to unpack them."

"Actually," I said, "I'd like to unpack them myself. If that's okay."

"Oh?" she looked at me quizzically.

I was glad she seemed intrigued. I wanted one person who worked here to know why my child's name was listed in their library's newest collection. So I told her how I wanted to do something special to remember Carly.

"What a wonderful way to commemorate your daughter." She smiled and led me down the hall to the children's room, gesturing to the bookshelves. "Take your time," she said.

The room was small with a colorful braided rug in the center. Light streamed through the sheer curtains covering the windows, making the yellow walls almost glow. Under one of the windows sat several trunks and large plastic bins filled with assorted toys: matchbox cars, plastic balls, Legos. Tiny wooden chairs surrounded small, round tables, and built-in shelves lined one wall holding a haphazard collection of books. They were stacked in no particular order and were well used, a torn page here, a bent cover there. *Perfect*, I thought. *This place needs an update.*

I planted myself on the floor and emptied my boxes. One by one I placed each book on a shelf, scattering them throughout the collection rather than in one clump. I figured more people would stumble upon Carly's books if I sprinkled them here and there. Occasionally, I opened the front cover of a particularly beloved book and looked at the lavender scrolls surrounding Carly's name on the bookplates. *So pretty*, I thought, hoping others would feel the same.

Driving back toward my new lakeside home, empty boxes in the backseat, I stopped at a favorite coffee shop and treated myself to hot cocoa. At my table bathed in late morning sunshine, I savored each sip of the velvety warm chocolate and imagined a day in the future when a young mother might be staying at the Ronald McDonald House. Perhaps one of her children would be recovering from surgery at the nearby hospital while she rested at a table with her healthy child and a copy of *The Hungry Caterpillar*. She'd stare for a moment at the bookplate so carefully placed inside. She would wonder about this child named Carly: How did she die? How old would she be now? She would pull her boy into her lap, kiss his cheek, and wrap her arms around his waist. And after he nagged her to read the book, she'd send a silent prayer to her ill son, to Carly, and to Carly's mom. Then she'd turn the page and begin reading.

My wandering mind turned to the scene in the coffee shop's parking lot: a poplar tree's bare branches filled with a flock of warbling finches, squirrels scampering through its dried-up leaves below, and two chubby toddlers dashing around their mother's legs while she fiddled with her car keys. An unexpected gush of affection washed over me. For the achingly cute children playing wholeheartedly. For the finches singing earnestly above them. For how good the warm mug of hot cocoa felt inside my cupped hands. For the shimmering sunbeam brightening the table. In that moment, the entire universe was the coffee shop, and it was joyful and welcoming and alive. And I was a part of it.

Chapter 41—CUSP

B ooks delivered, I puttered around my new home for the rest
of the day and finished unpacking. I stacked linens in a small
closet, filled desk drawers with pens and paper, and displayed vases
and candles on bookshelves. The place started to feel cozy. One
small carton remained, and I brought it to my bedroom where the
late afternoon sun spread patches of light across the cornflower
blue walls. I carefully unwrapped all the contents and laid them on
my bed. There was the pink ceramic bowl holding Carly's hospital
ID bracelet, her ultrasound picture, and several shells from my
trip to Florida. There was also the birch picture frame with a copy
of Carly's footprints behind the glass, the eggplant journal—the
first I'd filled, the floral hatbox brimming with sympathy cards,
her photo. The bedroom boasted deep windowsills, and with the
wide lawn rolling to the lake as a backdrop, I chose them as the
home for my keepsakes of Carly. I placed each memento carefully
along the sill, and this is where they remained for the two years I
would live in that apartment.

Near sunset, after tearing down the last of the boxes, I threw
on my coat, wrapped a scarf around my neck, and walked down
to the dock. The wintry air filled my lungs, and the wind rippled

the water. I thought about the whirlwind of the last year: Carly's death, family wedding, miscarriage, split from Jason, new teaching gig, and a move to a different home. And of course, marking Carly's first anniversary. Reaching this landmark birthday had weighed on me as an important milestone to bear, and anniversaries beyond the first seemed so far in the future. I never considered them as events I'd need to endure.

I was wrong. I've learned that as I tick them off, I can expect a mood shift in the weeks before. Tenderness sets in from the sight of a vibrant winter sunset or the refrain from a far-off mourning dove. That sore spot in my heart rises to the surface as I imagine a growing Carly. Age three: Chubby little hands stacking blocks. Age five: Kindergarten! First lunch box! Age eight: Reading like crazy. Age twelve: A leggy pre-teen.

I can also expect a letter from Jennifer. We write each other yearly on our respective anniversaries to muse about our missing babies and to express deep appreciation for finding kindred spirits in each other. We continue to walk the journey together.

I didn't know any of this, of course, as I stared into the gloaming sky and the charcoal-dyed lake. Sinking deeper into the bench, I tightened my scarf and hugged my arms around my torso with each gust of chilly wind. Even though my skin stung against the biting temperature, each breath relaxed my body more, compelling me to remain on the dock.

That night was the first of many I'd gaze out at the lake's ever-changing tableau, and as the months passed, the tranquil setting began to breathe new life in me. My bearings had been lost for so long, starting with my impulsive departure from Boston and then intensifying over the two and a half years that followed. By the time I landed in the lakeside apartment, I hungrily soaked up my surrounding's boundless beauty and savored the peace and quiet. Whether relaxing at the water's edge, among pink and ivory roses on the patio, or in front of the crackling fireplace on a frosty night, I grew more peaceful. Sometimes Carly would seem as close and dear as a nesting bluebird in the wooden box affixed to a soaring pine, or the elegant drape of the willow tree's limbs, or the sparkles of light bouncing across the water. I relished the connection I felt in those moments, not just to her, but also to the splendor of the entire landscape.

Spending time in the lush outdoors was one curative I discovered at the lake house. The other was solitude, and my relationship to it transformed as I settled into my new life. In the year after Carly's death, I had plenty of alone time, though it seemed an imperative, not a choice. The early shock and despair of losing Carly had sapped my energy, and being around others for too long was simply overly taxing. Later, yearning to bond with my spirit daughter was a solo quest requiring me to push everything and everyone aside. After Jason left, the initial period of living alone was a relief, because I no longer had to live with the drama and turmoil of our deteriorated relationship. Finally, I moved to the lake house where I was no longer laden with crippling grief or problems to solve. I could just be. In this newfound freedom, I embraced solitude not as a means to survive, but as a way to thrive. Loneliness is an aching void, but solitude, I came to understand, is a nourishing renewal. I could unclutter my mind and restore equanimity by taking myself for a long walk under the canopy of trees in my verdant new neighborhood, or lounging all day with a good book, or piling yarn on my lap to knit my way through a rented movie. Living at the lake house gave me many gifts, but perhaps the greatest of all was learning to tap into a wellspring of deep contentment found within solitude.

The longing for what might have been could still hit me like a gut punch—my sorrow as thick and heavy as lead shroud—and I'd fall into my sofa or take myself out to the dock where I'd sit and sit and sit. But I grew to trust that these periods of paralysis would eventually end and that I'd often feel lighter afterward, as if bearing the pain softened the edges of everything around and inside of me, making room for peace.

That first evening on the dock gave me a taste of what lay ahead. Lights from homes across the lake twinkled in the now inky sky, and if it weren't for a gnawing hunger, I might have stayed out all night, savoring the placid state of my body and mind. But I pushed myself off the bench and turned to face my new home. The glow from the fireplace illuminated the windows, and I could make out my cats' silhouettes sitting along the sofa's back. I knew that for the rest of the evening, I'd do nothing more than sip a bowl of soup, listen to music, and cozy up with my cats. It would be a perfect end to the day.

I turned to the lake one last time, closed my eyes and whispered into the faint wind, "My sweet Carly, do you see me? Can you hear me? You're my girl. Always."

EPILOGUE

The stories came in steadily.

One friend gave twenty dollars to a barista at a local coffee shop with instructions to gift customers free drinks until the money ran out. Another friend left a bouquet of flowers at her neighbor's front door. Another volunteered at a homeless shelter. My niece and nephew passed out chocolates to each of their class-mates. My brother helped a colleague install new kitchen cabinets, and my sister-in-law delivered poinsettias to friends, just because. My mother surprised a sick neighbor with groceries.

Each year on Carly's birthday, I prepare a special activity in her honor: pizza and cupcakes with friends, a cup of coffee with a lonely acquaintance, cookies for maternity staff in the hospital. For what would have been Carly's tenth birthday, I invited others to carry out a random good deed in her memory and was delighted by the creative and generous endeavors delivered to me via photos and narratives. I assembled and sent friends and family a digital album of snapshots and stories of acts of kindness. It felt good to share Carly's birthday tributes with those who had supported me in those early years.

And it felt good to reflect. As I do annually, I stayed home on Carly's birthday and indulged in my remembrance ritual. I lit a candle, listened to the same CD played during Carly's delivery, sorted through her memorabilia, and wrote her a letter. I keep a special journal of letters just for her where I share the happenings in my life and imagine what she would be up to had she lived. (The journal itself was a gift from Jason back when I was pregnant. Its delicate pages are handmade, the binding is stitched with ribbon, and we'd planned to use it as a memory book for our baby's first year. Despite my bitter ending with Jason, writing yearly in this particularly elegant journal is my gesture of goodwill to Carly's father.) The tenth anniversary gave me plenty to write about, not just the wonderful array of good deeds carried out in her name, but also the many changes in the last decade. I was not the same woman I'd been when I first lost her.

Settling and recuperating in the lake house provided fertile ground to grow new roots and allowed me to reach out and make connections in the community. Where I once had only family and a few work associates in my Chapel Hill circle and a general uncertainty about where I fit in, I gradually created a network of supportive confidantes to hike, dine, and talk with. A writing group that I joined in those early years gave me the intimate space and unconditional acceptance to tell my story; the bond forged with my writing sisters endures. I befriended neighbors and fellow practitioners at a meditation center. And while I'm still close to a few New England friends, I'm more fully tied to the life I built for myself in North Carolina.

My department at the university exploded with opportunities, and I seized them. My responsibilities expanded when my position became full time, as did my salary, enabling me to take the lead on interesting and fulfilling projects and to stop counting each nickel. I am more engaged, challenged, and invested than ever before, even when at the height of my teaching career.

A few years after Jason and I split, I dipped my toe back into the dating pool with much more care and caution, and only with a breed of man who is settled and steady, and whose heart is generous and secure. I was with someone for five happy years, and we shared a home and friends and the ultimate realization that we could no longer grow together. Our separation was tender and loving. While I continue to date and hope for a lifelong partner, the yearning is not laced with pressure. I understand now that the most significant relationship to cultivate is with myself. And with you, Carly.

I will always miss you. Even now I can feel the sting of losing you when I see mothers and daughters together. Sometimes their bond is so plainly obvious, like in the way they wander absent-mindedly through the aisles of a store, half-talking, half-listening, yet somehow fully attuned with the other. They seem to reside in a private bubble that will keep them forever joined no matter how far apart their paths may take them.

You never felt the sunshine on your face, never savored the scent of a magnolia blossom, and never took a breath outside of me. But Carly, I believe we are still together, and I can feel the many blessings you've given me. Had we been swept along in the day-to-day routines and demands of family life, would I have sought a more simple way of being and developed a spiritual curiosity? Instead of mindlessly rushing through the mornings readying myself for work as I'd done for years, would I awaken early to meditate or practice yoga or simply sit on my deck listening to birdsongs? Walking through a wooded trail on a fall afternoon, I stop and gaze at the last traces of sunlight casting a magical glow to auburn and golden leaves. Inexplicably, I feel awash in peace. I know moments like these are gifts from you, as if you're right there, guiding me to look beyond myself to find beauty and mystery. And I know you're near when in the middle of a spring day packed with meetings and email, something compels me to pause and glance out my office window. Fresh buds on the young maple tree in the courtyard below, laughter from a pair of college students walking past, a sparrow alit on the ledge of my windowsill. Life abounds. I close my eyes and send you gratitude for helping me breathe it all in.

ACKNOWLEDGMENTS

In the early months after Carly's death, journaling became a sort of salvation. I'd always kept journals, but writing became more urgent while I walked forward in my disorienting new world. About a year into my persistent journaling, I'd discovered that Carol Henderson, author of *Losing Malcolm* and *Farther Along*, was leading a new writing group in Chapel Hill, and I joined. Initially, I rarely shared any pieces about Carly but instead honed my writing skills on light-hearted topics. Over time, the group eventually settled into a core set of five women, and we stuck together for years. It was in the company and comfort of these particular women that I started sharing writing about Carly, and soon my full story started to flow. Without question, I could not have written *From the Lake House* without this group. Carol Henderson, with her intuitive listening and keen eye, saw the makings of a memoir before I did. Carolyn Cooper, Mairead Eastin Moloney, Susie Wilde, and Nancy Tilly were beyond generous and insightful in helping me sharpen and polish each and every draft. I have deep gratitude for each of these women, who are gifted writers and cherished friends.

I'm also indebted to my family, who lifted me up and kept me afloat during the first year. I had the incredible fortune of living on the same street as my brother David and sister-in-law Kate, whose steady presence and generosity gave my days immeasurable bright spots. My mother picked up countless phone calls from me, listened attentively, and somehow made me feel as if the ground beneath my feet would once again be solid. The rest of my family visited and also cared for me from afar, reminding me that physical distance cannot diminish support or love.

Jennifer Soos is a dear and special friend, and I will always be grateful to the MISS Foundation for their online support forum, where Jennifer and I first connected. Though we've never met in person, Jennifer and I have a unique bond. Our email correspondence sustained me in the year after Carly's death, and I cannot imagine enduring the raw days of grief without walking virtually beside Jennifer. In writing this memoir, I mined our reams of emails for memories and feelings from that time period; those letters between two grieving mothers provided invaluable material. Our lives are wholly different now than when we first met, but Jennifer and I still write annually to each other and still share the indefinable sadness of missing children we never got to know. My heart is filled with appreciation for the many gifts I received during that difficult season in my life; my friendship with Jennifer is among my most treasured.

Though he's no longer living, I'm indebted to my therapist, Victor Zinn, who played a much larger role in my life than is conveyed in my book. Victor radiated patience, wisdom, and compassion, and sitting with him each week was like visiting an oasis. Victor helped me find words for my sorrow, and to experience grief not just as a loss but also as sacred and holy work.

Carly's father deserves acknowledgment. We were poorly matched and not nearly strong enough to endure our loss and stay together, but I know we did our best. And though we've long since lost contact, he and I will be forever linked through Carly. Losing her was transformative and has ultimately blessed me in many ways, and I recognize that her father is inextricably part of this equation.

Finally, many thanks to the fabulous team at She Writes Press for shepherding me through the publication process. For a long time, the idea of publishing my memoir seemed daunting, and I kept From the Lake House tucked away in my computer for several years. Thanks to the nudging of several friends, I finally searched for a publisher, and I am delighted to have landed with She Writes Press. The community of supportive staff and fellow authors has assured me that I found the right home for my memoir.

ABOUT THE AUTHOR

K risten Rademacher has lived in Chapel Hill, North Carolina, since 2002, which is when she began writing. *From the Lake House* is her first memoir. She holds a master's degree in education and life coach certification. Rademacher is an Academic Coach at the University of North Carolina at Chapel Hill.

Author photo © Christy Clemons

SELECTED TITLES FROM SHE WRITES PRESS

She Writes Press is an independent publishing company founded to serve women writers everywhere. Visit us at www.shewritespress.com.

Expecting Sunshine: A Journey of Grief, Healing, and Pregnancy after Loss by Alexis Marie Chute. $16.95, 978-1-63152-174-4. A mother's inspiring story of surviving pregnancy following the death of one of her children at birth.

Breathe: A Memoir of Motherhood, Grief, and Family Conflict by Kelly Kittel. $16.95, 978-1-938314-78-0. A mother's heartbreaking account of losing two sons in the span of nine months—and learning, despite all the obstacles in her way, to find joy in life again.

Three Minus One: Parents' Stories of Love & Loss edited by Sean Hanish and Brooke Warner. $17.95, 978-1-938314-80-3. A collection of stories and artwork by parents who have suffered child loss that offers insight into this unique and devastating experience.

Rethinking Possible: A Memoir of Resilience by Rebecca Faye Smith Galli. $16.95, 978-1-63152-220-8. After her brother's devastatingly young death tears her world apart, Becky Galli embarks upon a quest to recreate the sense of family she's lost—and learns about healing and the transformational power of love over loss along the way.

Filling Her Shoes: Memoir of an Inherited Family by Betsy Graziani Fasbinder. $16.95, 978-1-63152-198-0. A "sweet-bitter" story of how, with tenderness as their guide, a family formed in the wake of loss and learned that joy and grief can be entwined cohabitants in our lives.

Of This Much I'm Sure: A Memoir by Nadine Kenney Johnstone. $16.95, 978-1631522109. After an IVF procedure leads to near-fatal internal bleeding, Nadine Kenney Johnstone must ask herself if the journey to create life is worth risking her own—and eventually learns that in an unpredictable life, the only thing she can be sure of is the healing power of hope.